How Great Golfers Think

How Great Golfers Think

PERFECTING YOUR MENTAL GAME

Bob Skura

Bob Skura & Company Inc.

Library and Archives Canada Cataloguing in Publication

Skura, Bob, 1950 –

ISBN 978-0-9784063-0-1

1. Golf – Mental game   2. Success   3. Instruction   I. Title.

Editors: Fina Scroppo and Suzanne Moutis
Consultant and coordinator: Fina Scroppo
Design, page layout and print production: www.wemakebooks.ca

Although the author has exhaustively researched all sources to ensure the accuracy and completeness of the information contained in this book, we assume no responsibility for errors, inaccuracies, omissions, or any inconsistency herein. Any slights of people or organizations are unintentional.
All of the characters in this book are fictitious. Any resemblance to actual persons, living or dead, is purely coincidental.

Address all inquiries to:

Bob Skura & Company Inc.
127 Woodview Cres.
Kitchener, ON, Canada
N2A 3E5
doc@howgreatgolfersthink.com
www.howgreatgolfersthink.com/

Printed in Canada

To my father,
who encouraged me to believe
almost anything is possible.

And to my mother,
who led me to believe
all of us have vast potential to develop.

ACKNOWLEDGMENTS

I want to thank the University of Waterloo on many different levels. I received my post-secondary education there and had the opportunity to play golf for the school. It's also the home of the library where much of the research for this book was done. Many people key to the success of *How Great Golfers Think* have an affiliation with the school. One such person is psychology professor Rich Ennis, PhD, who evaluated the book for accepted principles of his discipline and offered valuable insight. Jack Pearse and Dave Hollinger, both very much a part of the university's culture of excellence, are past and present coaches of the Waterloo Warrior golf teams respectively. Every year a new crop of players puts their talents on display, but I was especially privileged to get to know the 2005 Waterloo Warrior golf team personally. The members helped me develop fresh ideas during presentations I made to them as a prelude to writing this book. Finally, many University of Waterloo alumni contributed to this book in one way or another.

My wife, Sharon, deserves special thanks for her unwavering support. She constantly shielded me from distractions so that I could concentrate on writing.

Six people became my virtual traveling companions on the journey to produce this book. The first two were my talented editors, Fina Scroppo and Suzanne Moutis. Not only are they wonderful people, but also they guided me in maintaining my own voice while adhering to sound writing principles. The other four were Larry Anstett, David Chilton, Pete McMenemy and Jerry Wright, personal friends, golfers and high achievers in their own rights. They put up with my frequent phone calls and intrusions into their everyday lives as I sought feedback at various stages of this project.

Thank you to those who assisted in the proofreading and in the exchange of ideas. Some may not even have known they were contributing to a book when they provided me with advice, speaking opportunities and contacts. My thanks go to: Dianne Amy, Stephanie Bear, Matt Beechey, John Carter, Steve Chiasson, Bill Duffy, Chris Elliott, Justin Fluit, William Gilmore, Jamie Gregg, Patty Howard, Oliver Jahn, Steve Johnson, Marg Koop, Terry Lalande, Mark Lang, David Lea, Greg Lee, Ross MacDonald, Jim Malcolmson, Mike Martz, David Mathers, Don McCrae, Scott McRae, Dave Minnes, Jonathan Minnes, Sandi Minnes, Robbie Moore, Aimee Oliverio, Ron Pearson, Ken Pitman, Janet Podleski, Isabel Price, Mark Pus, Mark Quinn, Dean Salter, Mark Schram, Mike Silver, Harry Skura, Mary Skura, Mac Voisin, Arjun Walia and Jud Whiteside.

Finally, thank you to my brainstorming group. I tested various titles and covers through the convenience of e-mail, bringing people together in a virtual room over the course of a few weeks. The candid input of the following people was very much appreciated: Bowie Abbis-Mills, Bill Appleby, Rick Baxter, Dennis Black, Bill

Bodfield, Bob Brehl, Drew Brown, Bob Cadman, Bruce Clarke, Dino Constable, Jay Cressman, Kelvin Day, Mike Dohaney, Steve Elgee, Chris Elliott, Brian Fisher, Rob Fitzpatrick, Barry Gillespie, Jim Gruber, John Harrigan, Ed Heakes, Jim Highendman, Rachel Hoffman, Bill Hutchison, Paul Ingram, Gordon Jennings, John Kabucis, Gail Kennedy, Paul Knight, Jeff Knudsen, Ken Koss, Bob Leadley, Jeff Legault, Art Linton, Brian Lipskie, Jeremy Logel, Bob Love, John MacTavish, Tim McCutcheon, Don McLean, Duncan McLean, Derek Mercey, Joan Moore, Ben Moser, Doug Painter, Alan Paleczny, Glenn Peister, Randy Potipcoe, Kent Potts, Johnathan Rigby, Joe Robertson, Graham Ross, Lou Roussy, Chris Skura, Mike Skura, Les Smith, Bob Stephens, Peter Temple, John Thompson, Anton Verhoeven, Elaine Voisin, Andy Watson, Brian White, Fred Wilder and Bruce Wilson.

At every stage, the opinions of these people were invaluable. They made writing the book humbling, but more rewarding. And, I am certain that in the end, they contributed to a better product for the reader.

My thanks to all.

Bob Skura

CONTENTS

ABOUT THIS BOOK

Almost unanimously, the people who read early drafts of this book requested a chapter-by-chapter **summary of the key points for easy reference. In order to accommodate that request and still maintain literary flow, certain portions of text are highlighted in bold.** This format allows you to get the most out of the book while enjoying its story line without interruption.

That being said, the story you are about to read is a journey of mental skill development for both your sporting and everyday lives. Along the way, you'll read how the main characters are exposed to the ideas of world-renowned psychologists like Edwin Locke and Gary Latham (goal-setting), Mihaly Csikszentmihalyi (known as the Guru of Flow), D.H. Meichenbaum (SIT – Stress Inoculation Training), Maria Montessori (childhood education), Lev Vygotsky (an expert on the function of language in human development), Carol S. Dweck (personality and social development) and Albert Bandura (the third most frequently cited psychologist in introductory psychology textbooks after Sigmund Freud and B.F. Skinner).

There are great thinkers in every field of achievement, but we are golfers, so stories about Tiger Woods, Jack Nicklaus and other famous professionals are used frequently to illustrate how they apply the fundamentals of success.

I chose to use conversations between realistic, though fictional, golfers in an imaginary setting so that the book's lessons come across as a story line rather than a lecture. Also, the endnotes have been designed to be more than academic references. They not only source the psychology literature behind the lessons, but also include short, easy-to-read excerpts that further your understanding of key principles.

However, regardless of the format, the message I want to convey is a simple one: Whatever your stage in life, learning new skills can be relatively easy. As a result, you'll enjoy a more satisfying and productive life.

CHAPTER 1

GOLF'S MENTALLY ILLITERATE

"Where's the scorecard?" grumbled Andy.

"Frank's got it, and he's in the shower," Kip said, trying to hold back a smile.

"I hope he's washing away his bad shots," Andy wisecracked. "I think we lost all the bets to you and Jason today."

Every Saturday morning for the past two seasons, Kip, Jason, Andy and Frank have played 18 holes together at the River Bend Golf Club in Aurora, Ohio, a beautiful university town on the outskirts of Cincinnati. Afterward there are usually a few bets to settle over a light meal. However, this Saturday was different; it was the Saturday of Masters Weekend, the official start of the season for most golfers, bringing with it hope for rebirth on the golf course. Frank appeared from the locker room, his graying hair still wet, and joined the others. He flicked the foursome's scorecard onto the table and with an audible sigh slumped into a chair. "Good grief. That was a rough day."

Kip took the card and started tallying it up, while Jason angled his lanky body so that he could see over his friend's shoulder. "According to this," said Kip, "we won the front, the back and the overall. Plus you pressed us once. Dig deep, guys. That makes it four ways."

"Big deal. We'll get most of it back," replied Andy. "The winners have to buy the drinks."

"Yeah, one of these days we should change that tradition," Kip chuckled. "I can't win for losing."

A natural talent and determined to achieve, Kip Raston is the glue that holds this group together for the simple reason that he's the best golfer of the four. At 24 years old, he's a successful sales rep for an industrial parts manufacturer, a job he's held since graduating from a Big Ten college, where he captained the golf team. Yet even though he had an impressive college record, Kip has never won a national competition or even one outside his own state. With an athletic, 175-pound body enhanced by a faithful exercise routine, he has all the physical attributes to succeed. But Kip feels his full potential is held back by the lack of a mental skill he can't quite put his finger on. Nevertheless, Kip's game is a treat to behold. On the days he really gets it going, his friends just watch his shots and shake their heads in awe.

Frank was staring at the table now with the frustrated look that a bogey, bogey, bogey finish tends to cause. "I guess it's hard to teach an old dog new tricks," he said, shaking his head. "You know, I've played golf for 45 years. I know more about the game than I ever did, and my scores still go up. What does it take to get better at this stupid game?"

A 58-year-old recently retired teacher, Frank is a walking golf encyclopedia. Given that his parents impressed the value of schooling on him, that's no surprise. He's tried almost every swing technique ever taught, and carries an eight handicap, though at one time it was considerably lower. Over the past few years, the frustrations of the game have eroded his enthusiasm, just at a time in life when he has the opportunity to enjoy golf most. He tries to put on a brave face, but for him the sport isn't what it once was. In fact, if it weren't for the energy he absorbs from playing with these friends on Saturdays, he probably would be playing very little golf.

Jason saw an opportunity to egg Frank on. "I thought you said you had it all figured out on the range this morning. To hear you tell it, you were striping it like Fred Funk, but you ended up playing like Freddy Flop."

"Very funny, hotshot, but as I recall, you had it under par for a while, then turned a 71 into a 75. You can't be happy with that score."

Frank's comment hit a nerve. "Yeah, I think maybe I need another lesson," Jason conceded, becoming a bit quieter.

Jason is a typical 17-year-old. He's excited about his future and naturally confident that he can do almost anything, yet occasionally anxious, wondering if his dreams really will come true. All the same, he's talented. Jason's rapidly improving game over the past year has brought his handicap down to zero – two behind Kip's plus two.[1] Since he's nearing the end of his junior career, his talent, plus his above-average size, make him a big fish in a small pond. So he's trying to win everything he can in his age group before moving on to the next level.

"#@%! the lessons. Just go out there and have a good time. That's the way I play," Andy proclaimed, raising his glass. "By the way, boys, thanks for the drink!"

Andy is one of a kind. Thirty-nine years old and nurturing a solid spare tire around his middle – "a low center of gravity," in his words – he's the owner of a roofing company. Golf-wise, he's a 14 handicap and claims to be very serious about the game, but really only shows it for the split second it takes him to swing a club. The rest of the time, Andy's usually looking for some way to keep the mood of the group lighthearted, and he generally succeeds.

"Hah!" Frank responded. "You play for the fun of it, do you, Mr. Volcano? Just how many clubs has fun-loving Andy broken so far this year? As I recall, you snapped your driver over your knee on your winter vacation. Then, in your first game back home, you threw your five-iron into never-never land, and just last week you mortally wounded your putter. Some fun, huh?"

"Sounds like our Andy all right," Kip chuckled. "But you know, besides the lessons we've invested in, I bet we could start a pretty good retail outlet with all the clubs, books, videos and swing aids we've bought over the years. And tell me: Have any of them actually helped?"

"How come you're trashing swing aids and instruction magazines? I think they're awesome," Jason countered. "Isn't that why all the players are so good these days?"

"Okay, so they help some people," conceded Kip. "But why aren't guys like us improving more? Like Frank said, we learn more about the game and swing mechanics every day, yet after the age of about 21 or 25, the average player doesn't seem to get *that* much better. I wouldn't say I'm slipping, but I've sure noticed that my improvement has started to level off in the past year or two. The swing aids are helping you now, but probably anything would help at your age. I think we need something more, and I think there's something extra to help you too. You could use a better mental approach. You've even told me so!"

"Forget about it," Andy persisted. "You guys are going about it all wrong. Just ante up for a new driver every spring and buy yourself a game. I wouldn't go in for any of that brainy stuff."

"Brainy stuff? No kidding, partner!" Frank smirked. "Your 95 today certainly wasn't too brainy for a 14 handicap. It's a good thing I'm not your partner every week. I'd go broke."

"Who's worried? I've got lots of room to improve," Andy grinned. "Kipster here beat me by 25 shots today. He's so good he doesn't have anything to look forward to."

Kip dismissed Andy's comment with a wave of his hand. "Huh! You think we're that good, do you? Jason and I won the bets today, but my game wasn't anything to write home about considering how easy the course played. We're just fortunate that the way you guys slapped it around, we could've beaten you with a couple of brooms, an apple and an orange."

"I don't know what you're complaining about, Kip," Jason said with surprise. "With the scores you shoot and the tournaments you've won, what else do you want?"

Kip looked off into the distance, as if trying to bring some internal image into focus. "You know what I really want, Jason?" Kip said slowly. "I really want to play in the Masters!"

With his drink stopped halfway to his open mouth, Frank slowly turned toward Kip. "*You* want to play in the Masters? *You?*"

Andy had a less subtle response. "Buddy, there's more chance of me being elected president of the United States than you playing in the Masters, and my chances are zero. Although, in my case, it's not lack of ability. People just aren't ready for my razor-sharp mind."

"That would be awesome, Kip," said a wide-eyed Jason. "But how would you ever get into that tournament?"

"A lot of people forget," explained Kip, "that a nonprofessional can earn a spot in the Masters through the U.S. Amateur. The winner and runner-up traditionally get an invitation to play in the Masters the following spring."

Kip smiled and turned toward the group's jester. "That gives me two chances every year to do what I want to do, Andy, while you could only be elected president once every four years. You know, I could win the Amateur, do the talk-show circuit, and be back in time to organize your presidential campaign. How would you like that?"

Without waiting for an answer Kip turned back to the others. "Let's face it, every amateur dreams of playing at Augusta one way or another. Every professional wants to get there, too, and win, to be immortalized in the history of the game. Can you just imagine what it would feel like driving up Magnolia Lane toward the clubhouse? They'd put you up in the Crow's Nest,[2] where Palmer, Nicklaus and Woods stayed as amateurs. Then you'd get to tee it up in the tournament. Man, I'm telling you, that would be like dying and going to heaven."

Frank and Andy were noticeably less skeptical than before, while Jason, awed at the possibility, kept pressing for how such a dream could come true. "It would be fantastic just to know someone who played in it. What do you think you'd have to do to finish first or second in the U.S. Amateur and get invited?"

"Obviously, I'd have to play better than I do now – a lot better! My approach to the game has to be different too. I've been thinking about this a lot lately, and I've decided I need some out-of-the-box thinking. After all, that's how breakthroughs seem to come about in the business world."

Kip leaned forward in his chair. "From what I understand, nylon stockings weren't invented by the hosiery industry. They were invented by DuPont, which was an explosives company until it got into chemical research."

"You've lost me," said Frank, pausing to put his glass down. "What does that approach have to do with golf?"

"Lots," Kip replied. "The best golfers of all time thought outside the box too. Hogan practiced when everyone else just warmed up. Nicklaus was pacing off yardages when everyone was guessing at distances. These days we have Tiger proving that physical conditioning isn't only for football players."

Then, speaking very deliberately to make a key point, Kip said, "Someone should take ideas from psychology, teaching, business, self-improvement, plus who knows what other disciplines, apply them to the mental side of golf instruction and take it to a whole new level. That would be thinking outside the box. If I ever find a person who does that, I'm going to sit on his doorstep until he teaches me everything he knows."

"What's caused this sudden burst of thinking, Kip?" asked Frank. "Like Jason said, I thought you were pretty happy with your game."

"Oh, I've thought about it before, but what got me thinking about a higher level lately was something I came across in a magazine the other day. The article was called "How Mentally Literate Is Your Golf Game?" It had a quiz in it. I don't remember the name of the guy who wrote it, except that he had a short nickname, like someone you'd expect had been at the books for a while. Anyway, I can't resist a challenge, so I picked up a pen and started trying to answer questions like: How can you improve your self-talk? How do you build a strong self-image? What do top-ranked athletes do to get into the zone?

"I tell you, not only was I unhappy with the answers I came up with, but I also realized I don't even think along those lines. After going through the questions, I was really frustrated. It's not that I expect to play like Tiger Woods every day. I'd just like to borrow his talent for a tournament or two. And if I could answer those questions better, I bet I could make a real breakthrough because then I'd have the tools I need." The others were listening intently now, and nodding their heads as Kip's ideas began to take shape. "I think every golfer feels the same way. We all hope to discover the magic secret that'll lift us to another level, but how's that ever going to happen if we keep doing the same things today that we did yesterday? **We need a two-pronged approach — both physical *and* mental improvement — if we want to get better.** The best swing lessons in the world won't do it on their own."

Andy became more serious than usual, exposing a hint of vulnerability. "Not a bad point, Kip. I might buy into this mental stuff if it could get rid of my slice. Can you guarantee me that?"

Leaning close, Kip replied in a near whisper. "I'm not sure about helping it, but I can guarantee you this…"

"What?" Andy said, also leaning in.

"…nothing could hurt it!" Kip boomed, slapping Andy on the back.

Andy recoiled and frowned at his sparring partner. "You know, you should show me more respect. I'm older than you are."

"Aye, aye, Sir. From now on I will," Kip promised unconvincingly. "Seriously, though, playing in the Masters might be a stretch, but what if? Even if there's only an outside chance to get there, it has to be worth a try. There's nothing to lose."

"You know, Kip, you're smarter than you look," Frank teased. "If I think back, I used to tell my students something along those same lines. I'd say to them that there was something special in all of us. I could just as well have said, there's a 'Masters' in every one of us. Who knows what the key is for each individual, but there's probably a personal goal that can give each of us the fresh approach to the game we had when we were just starting to play. We just have to find it. Even our good buddy Andy here, with all his kidding around, knows it too."

"Hey, I appreciate that professor," replied Kip. "So how about some advice? If you were in my shoes what would you do? Where would you start?"

"Well, what none of us have probably ever done is gone to our pro and asked him for help with our mental game. Sure, we've tried to steal ideas from him from time to time, but we've never had a serious talk about it. Let's get Robbie Owen in here and see what he has to say. Maybe he can help us out."

Frank's idea seemed to make sense. After hearing his suggestion, Kip stood up. "That sounds like a great idea. I'm pretty sure Robbie's in the pro shop now. I'm going to tell him what we've been talking about, and see if he has time for a little chat."

CHAPTER 2

---◆---

AN UNEXPECTED REFERRAL

"Hey Robbie. I figured I'd find you here," Kip said cheerfully as he walked into the pro shop. "You got a moment?"

"Sure, Kip. What's up?" replied Robbie Owen, River Bend's golf pro. Robbie nodded and listened carefully as Kip summarized the conversation he'd been having with his golfing buddies and why they were interested in his input.

"So, have you got a few minutes to talk to us?" Kip asked.

"Sure! But I'll tell you what. I'm just finishing up my preparation for our charity Pro-Am this week, and if you give me half a minute to make sure I've got everything ready, I'll be done and we can talk all you want."

Robbie read through his checklist, item by item, and just loudly enough that Kip, still standing nearby, couldn't help but overhear. "Okay, the foursomes are all organized. I've got extra electric carts coming. Prizes? That leaves the prizes. Oh, right! I need one more set."

"Hey Robbie," said Kip, trying to be helpful. "It's really none of my business, but there's not a golfer in the world who needs another umbrella or a set of head covers. If it's a small prize you're looking for, see if you can rustle up something different for a change."

"You're right," Robbie replied. "I know the perfect thing! My shipment just came in." Robbie reached into a cabinet and pulled out four books, then set them beside the rest of the prizes. Job done. "Okay, Kip. Let's go."

The two men walked over to the table in the lounge where Jason, Andy and Frank were sitting. "Sounds like you've been having quite a conversation," commented Robbie. "How can I help?"

Everyone started speaking at once, until no one could be heard. Then all of a sudden everyone stopped and turned to Kip as if to say, "You ask him."

"Robbie, you're no stranger to competition," Kip began. "You shoot in the 60s quite often and you've won a bunch of local professional events. As I mentioned, our group is searching for a higher level of instruction. So, we'd like you to give us some lessons – but not regular lessons. We'd like some formal lessons on the mental approach to golf, because we think we're at a stage where that's what we need to improve."

"I'm surprised all four of you want help," kidded Robbie. "The Andy I know wouldn't agree to be part of this."

"Well, think of it as a trial run for him," Kip said with a grin. "In any case, how about the idea of mental lessons, Robbie?"

"Hey, I'm flattered you think I can offer that type of instruction, guys, but I'm afraid you'd be disappointed. I understand the importance of the mental part of the game, but I've never developed an organized lesson program I'd feel comfortable offering. I'd just be shooting from the hip."

The people at the table became noticeably more thoughtful. No one spoke for a moment, and then Robbie's eyes lit up. "Now that you mention it, though, I just might have what you need. Wait here a minute. I'll be right back."

As Robbie hurried off, Frank came to the support of his pro. "You know, maybe expecting Robbie to give us mental lessons was a bit far-fetched. His job here at River Bend is a handful in itself and on top of that, I hear he's doing some work with the University of Aurora golf team. He just wouldn't have the time."

"Yeah, you might be right," agreed Kip. "We'll have to see what he has up his sleeve."

"Here we are, guys," Robbie said, returning to the table with the four books he had put aside earlier as prizes. He handed a copy to each of the men. "This is for you, Kip. Here you are, Jason. One just for you, Frank, and one for you, Andy. Gentlemen, I believe this will give you the answers you're looking for."

Hardly glancing at the cover, Kip remarked, "Not that I don't appreciate your offer, Robbie, but I don't think another book is what we're after. Like I told you, we've tried all the golf gizmos. We've watched the videos and read the books, so what we really want is a personal touch. It would be better to have someone to talk to."

"This isn't just a book, guys," Robbie explained patiently. "As you'll see within the first few pages, it's an experience. It can be even more rewarding if you all read it at the same time, discuss it and help each other along."

"*The 3 Fundamentals of Success*," Jason read out loud. "Awesome. You'd think the author wrote the title after hearing what the four of us just talked about. So, is this a book about golf, Robbie, or a book about success?"

"It's both. You can read it to improve your golf game through a step-by-step application of the techniques that golf's greatest players used. Or, you can read it as a story, and apply its universal success principles to whatever you want to achieve. It all depends on which way you want to look at it, but it works either way."

"Sounds interesting. Who's the author and why are you so high on it?" asked Frank.

"It's written by someone I know named Doc, and the reason for my enthusiasm is I've seen the results. As you probably know, I've been affiliated with the University of Aurora golf team for the last few years. The team's coach wanted some assistance, so he asked me to help evaluate the players and offer some instruction. What you wouldn't know is that they've been working with this same fellow – Doc – to improve their mental game. Being part of the coaching staff, each year I've listened to the successful program he presents to the golf team. I say successful because the University of Aurora golf program has turned around completely since he's been associated with it. Sitting in on his presentations, I realized how much I didn't know about basic fundamentals of success. You know, guys, as much as I love being at this club, I honestly believe that I could have made it on tour if I'd been practicing Doc's fundamentals earlier in my career."

"Where have I heard that name before?" Kip asked, searching his memory. "Did you say his name is Doc?" Scratching his short wiry hair and looking once again at the author's name on the cover, he suddenly made the connection. "Yeah. That's the name of the guy who wrote the article I was telling you guys about earlier. Maybe we're closer to pay dirt than I thought."

"Doc's presentations include some pretty good stories,"

continued Robbie, "but they aren't just anecdotal. He's studied the research to validate his three fundamentals."

"What kind of research?" Frank wondered.

"May I see one of your books?" Robbie asked. Jason extended his arm across the table, offering his text. "Thanks, Jason. There are special notes in the back," said Robbie, flipping through the pages. "Yes, here they are." Then pointing to one of the author's endnotes, Robbie explained. "For example, we all know self-talk is important, but Doc used certain studies, like this one here, to prove that self-talk should include three components: task-specific content, affirmations and mood words.[3] In other words," Robbie said, putting down the book and looking at the men again, "when he spoke to us, he gave us the facts, not simply his personal opinions, or a rah-rah program. On top of that, he translated all those fancy studies into a language the players could understand.

"Anyway, after Doc's presentations to the team last fall, I was so impressed I told him he had to write the program down so other people could work through it. I suggested he break it up into a series of individual lessons, which he did. And now we've got *The 3 Fundamentals of Success*."

Frank still wanted more validation. "Fine, but what's his background?"

"Good question," replied Robbie. "Doc was a successful competitor from the day he began playing junior golf. Later on he won local invitations and a number of club championships. He's won at the state level and competed a few times in national events. Even now, at the age of 61, he's still winning the odd senior amateur event and posting a few rounds in the 60s every year, just like he has every year since he was a teenager."

Robbie paused for a moment to take a sip of the drink someone had ordered for him, and carried on. "Doc grew up on the West Coast, then came here to Aurora to get his degree. After a brief stint working in a pro shop and teaching lessons he opened up his own business, back on the coast, in the health-care industry. The nature of his work gave him hands-on experience in training people and helping them live up to their potential.

"From what he's told me, to improve his business skills, and to satisfy his personal curiosity, he made it a point throughout his life to study what makes people succeed. He'd get so involved in reading and research that his friends started calling him Doc, as in PhD."

"Sounds like a shrink to me," Andy said, eager to find a way into the conversation, "even if I haven't been on a couch since the last time I fell off a roof."

Jason looked over at Andy. "Someone told me you've actually fallen off three or four times. Is that really true?"

"Don't go there, buddy," Andy whispered. "Don't want my insurance agent to find out."

Robbie chuckled and went on. "A few years ago, a former player by the name of Jack Hollingsworth became coach of the University of Aurora golf team. It hadn't won a conference title since his days as a player, so he made a list of all the things he could do to improve its success. At the top of the list was a mentoring program for the present-day Aurora team, using as many of the former championship team members as possible. The thought being, players who were winners before could help the current team members be winners too.

"Doc was a star player, and a Hollingsworth teammate on those early championship teams. Right from the start of his involvement, it was obvious there was a mutual respect between him and the younger players. As a result, he offered to do some goal-setting for them based on his business experience, and it went well. Each year, he expanded his presentation to include new principles he had studied, and used, to help people become successful in the real world. And you know what? It worked! Three years ago, Aurora won its first conference title since the days when Doc and Hollingsworth played together."

Kip shifted anxiously in his chair. "That guy is using exactly the cross section of ideas we talked about before we invited you over, Robbie."

Robbie nodded to acknowledge Kip and continued. "Doc had been doing all this in conjunction with business trips to the area, but this past year he moved back here to Aurora permanently. That gave him a perfect opportunity to spend more time with the golf team. Last fall, U of Aurora won the conference title for the third time in a row, which you might know if you follow local sports. That's when I finally convinced him he had to write the program down for others to use."

Kip tapped his fingers rapidly on the tabletop. "I'm telling you, he's my kind of guy!"

"Hold on, Kip," requested Robbie. "I just have to tell you one more thing. "What you have in front of you is Doc's program. It contains nine main lessons, written in story form, with a main character offering reinforcement. Each lesson is designed to be read, and experienced, at one- or two-week intervals. You were a teacher, Frank. Learning something once or getting all pumped up by a motivational speech isn't nearly as effective, is it?"

Frank nodded in agreement. "People retain more when information is broken down into parts and they have the opportunity to integrate it into their routine over time. It also helps to have someone act as a reference point, someone who can reinforce the student and clarify confusing issues. Teachers, mentors, heros – call them what you want, they all play much the same role, and often provide the spark a person needs to really break out."

"Robbie, this is exactly what I've been looking for," Kip enthused as the others nodded eagerly. "But before I start reading the book, I'd really like to meet your friend Doc. Would that be possible?"

"Well, I hadn't thought of it, but actually, he lives just across the river," reflected Robbie. "He's even invited me over a few times."

"Hey that would be cool. I'd like to meet him too, " Jason said, not wanting to be left out. "It would be awesome to sit there and listen to someone like that."

"Might as well put me down too," said Andy. "The kid here needs a chaperon."

"I think what I'm hearing is that you all want to meet him and I guess there's no time like the present. Who's got a cell phone I can borrow?"

Within moments Robbie was holding a phone, had punched in a number, and was waiting for a response. "Hello, Doc, Robbie Owen over here at River Bend. How are you?…Good. Yes, the Masters is really starting to heat up. It looks like tomorrow's going to be interesting. My money's still on Tiger…. Could be! Anyway, Doc, I'm calling on behalf of a foursome of golfers. We were discussing your book as a way to help them develop the mental part of their games, and now they want to meet you, not just read what you've written. Do you think that would be possible?" Robbie was silent for a few moments as he listened to the answer.

"Just a second, I'll ask," Robbie held his hand over the speaker port and looked at the hopeful faces. "This is your lucky day. Doc says not only would he be willing to meet you since you're so keen, but he's been developing some new material, and would like to work through it with some live bodies. If you can be at his place tomorrow around 7 p.m., he'd be happy to discuss one lesson at a time with you, until you're finished going through his book."

"Absolutely," came a chorus of voices.

Robbie returned to the cell phone. "That works, Doc. They'll be there tomorrow. Yes, I'll tell them to bring their books along. Great talking to you, Doc, and thanks for your time. Bye for now. Bye."

"Well, what d'ya know, Jason? We're off to see Doc," said Andy, slapping the youngest member of the group on the back. "And it sounds like we're all going to need new hats after the stuff that guy's going to put in our heads. You know, I just might buy myself one of those big ten-gallon models. Always thought I'd look good in one of those."

Robbie laughed and gave the men directions to Doc's house before wrapping up the conversation and heading back to the pro shop. "You're all set, guys. You'll really enjoy Doc. He's a great guy and has a very interesting take on things."

"Hey, this is great. It's awfully good of you to put this together for us, Robbie. We really appreciate it," said Kip.

"Yeah," Frank agreed. "I'm looking forward to meeting this

Doc guy and getting started on the program. For me, it's a chance to clean out the cobwebs and rejuvenate myself. I need something like this."

"Okay guys," said Kip, taking on the task of organizing the group. "It sounds like his place is only about 10 minutes from here, so let's meet in the parking lot tomorrow at 6:45 p.m. That'll give us just enough time to finish watching the Masters before we leave to meet Doc."

CHAPTER 3

MEETING DOC

"Well, this is the address, guys," Kip declared as his vehicle arrived at a driveway in a quiet, park-like residential area. Kip slowed down and turned into the entrance, following the curving cobblestone until the car was parked in front of an elegant stone house nestled comfortably in the trees.

"Wow, is this ever a nice place," Kip exclaimed as the men got out of the car. "Those tall hardwoods frame the house like it's in a picture book. He's on the riverbank too. I bet we'll be able to see River Bend from the backyard.

"Welcome, fellows," a voice called out. It came from a man with a trim, six-foot frame and a smiling face. "I'm Doc," the gentleman said as he shook hands with each of the men, who introduced themselves in turn. After exchanging pleasantries, Doc made a suggestion. "Let's cut around the side, past the tool shed over here and sit in the backyard. It's a beautiful evening to sit outdoors."

In the time it took to walk to the backyard, the men traded information on their mutual friend Robbie Owen, and answered their host's question about refreshment preferences. As Doc disappeared into the house to get some drinks, the Saturday morning foursome took in their surroundings.

Jason whistled. "This is super. I bet you'd never grow tired of sitting here and looking out over a peaceful scene like this. Maybe when I make it on tour, I'll be able to buy a place just like it."

"I like the view Doc has from here," Kip remarked. "It looks like he's about 20 feet above the grade of the river and the golf course on the other side. It's just enough elevation to see really well."

"Here you are. Relax, and enjoy," Doc said as he set the beverages down on the patio table a few minutes later. "So, what did you fellows think of the Masters today?"

"Oh, it was amazing," Frank replied. "A nail-biter to the end, and I even won the pool, so life is good. It also looks like life's going to be good when we get into the program you've developed. Robbie said you've spent a lot of time studying the mental approach to golf and self-development."

"Well, you know, Frank, it started off fairly innocently. Early in my business career I was trying to make a point to someone by saying **You can climb any mountain if you just take one step at a time.** The person challenged me by saying those words were nothing more than motivational hype, and I wondered if he might be right, so I did some homework. I found out that there actually are studies to prove that breaking tasks into small portions improves performance.[4] Then I looked into some other ideas, and started connecting the dots and seeing how they applied to achievement in general. It turns out there's a fantastic amount of quality academic research around that hasn't yet been explained in the terms the everyday man on the street can digest easily."

"Is there anything that really surprised you?" Frank wondered.

"Lots of things, because you're learning all the time. If I had to pick one, though, the most surprising discovery I ever made is that getting into a zone, which, as you know, is what all athletes strive for, doesn't actually happen accidentally. While there's never a guarantee you can get into it on any given day, if you develop certain fundamental skills, you will be likely to have those peak experiences more often, and for longer periods of time. Not only that, but the principles of getting into the zone can also be applied in a way that enhances our everyday lives.

"In any case, one thing led to another. I got involved with the University of Aurora golf team, and that's how I met Robbie Owen. Both of us have enjoyed the progress we've seen in the players over the past few years."

"Right. We've noticed their success in the papers, but those university players have youth on their side, Doc," Frank pointed out. "Most of us – or at least I – don't have a future loaded with potential to look forward to." Then he chuckled self-consciously. "I want to play well, but I don't have the burning desire I once had. Are you sure you can do anything for a guy like me?"

"Excuse me. May I say something before you answer that, Doc?" Jason put in cautiously.

"Sure, go ahead."

"For me it's just the opposite. I look at successful golfers and people like you with this beautiful place, and I want to be successful too. I guess I feel confident about myself, but I don't even know what all of the things are that I'm supposed to learn, so I want you to teach me everything you can."

Doc enjoyed these contrasting points of view. "So one of you has burning desire, and the other only has a flicker left. Well, I like a challenge, so if you're willing to put in the work, I'm more than willing to match your effort. Despite Frank's concern, though, all of your futures are actually loaded with potential. In fact, you have more future than you have past. Let me ask you this. How old are each of you?"

The men told Doc that Kip was 24, Jason had just turned 17, Andy was 39, and Frank was the senior in the group at 58.

"What that means…hmmm, if we do the math…okay, considering your average life expectancy, you have 54, 61, 39 and 20 years of golf ahead of you, respectively. By those calculations, on average, there are more years of potential golfing enjoyment in your futures than in years already played. The determining factor in making progress and enjoying yourself from here on in is whether you move forward slightly more than you move backward. My job will be to get all of you to use proper mental skills 51 percent of the time. Moving forward for Frank would mean getting rid of that hint of pessimism I hear, one degree at a time. Helping Jason would be as simple as pointing his enthusiasm in the right direction and standing back to let him do his thing. For Kip, the objective would be to move steadily from uncertainty to confidence when he's going down the stretch. For Andy, it would be helping him bear down one more time, each round he plays."

"How'd you know all that about us?" Kip asked, impressed at how Doc had zeroed in on their weaknesses so quickly.

"Oh, I did my research," Doc smiled. "I talked to Robbie about you once more after he called yesterday."

"I thought you were going to say your job would be to get us to be positive 100 percent of the time," Kip said, still amazed.

"That's ideal in the long run," Doc replied, "but as they say, Rome wasn't built in a day."

"And you're certain you can even turn around an old dog like me?" Frank asked, seeking reassurance.

"It's easier than you think. Here's a brainteaser to prove it. A man is walking due east, and he alters his course by a single degree to the right, with one out of every 10 steps he takes. How far would he have to walk before he's walking in the opposite direction, or due west?"

"Elementary my dear Doc," replied Andy straight-faced. "Let it be known that you're looking at a human calculator here." Then, knowing full well he needed to buy more time to figure out the answer, he cleared his throat and waved his arms, priming himself for centre stage. "Aahhmm ahhhh mmm. The answer is one mile, and here's why. You need to turn 180 degrees to end up in the opposite direction. Since every 10 steps turns you one degree, taking 1,800 steps would turn you 180 degrees. We all know a step is about three feet, so the total is 5,400 feet, or roughly one mile. I know that, my good friends, because I play circular golf all the time. The trouble is, I don't know why Doc asked the question."

"That's because with all that multiplication you forgot to make a deduction," laughed Kip. "Obviously if we walk a mile with Doc, making small changes as we go, he'll turn us around."

"I knew that," quipped Andy.

Doc smiled at the antics of the men he was getting to know, and sensed that the coming weeks would be fun. "So, what it really comes down to is that **a steady application of sound**

fundamentals will get you anywhere you want to go. That's where The 3 Fundamentals of Success come in."

"Yeah, Doc. What are those three fundamentals? I've been dying to have you tell us about them," Kip asked impatiently.

"Kip, the 1st Fundamental of Success is How To Think. You can apply it, and the other fundamentals, to any discipline, which is what makes them so valuable."

"How To Think," Kip repeated slowly. "Doc, no disrespect, but isn't that a bit simple? I expected a little more to sink my teeth into. Something like: how to control my demons, how to trust my swing, or how to handle pressure."

"The simpler the better, Kip, although I understand where you're coming from. I'm sure Jason, Andy and Frank are thinking the very same thing, but rest assured, all of your concerns will be covered by the time we finish working through the three fundamentals. How To Think is about your goals and your self-image. We'll work on that fundamental first."

"Okay. I'll buy that," Kip replied. "So what are the other two fundamentals?"

"I hate to disappoint you, but you aren't ready for them yet. However, when you start to realize you need something more, you'll naturally ask new questions. That's when we'll move on to the next fundamental.

"And speaking of first things first, what single part of the golf swing has the greatest effect on the overall result? Would it be the address position, the start of the downswing, or something else?" asked Doc.

"The impact position," Andy guessed.

"Try again," Doc encouraged.

"Would it be the position at the top of the backswing?" ventured Jason.

"No."

"The first foot going back?" suggested Kip.

"Close."

"Come on, guys. Everyone knows the answer to that," said Frank. "It's the setup, or starting point. The things we do closest to the start of any activity have the greatest impact on the outcome."

"Frank's right," confirmed Doc. "In fact, Jack Nicklaus was a living example of the importance of a sound starting position. Even after he turned pro, he went to his instructor each spring for a refresher lesson on his grip, posture and alignment. Also, over every shot, in every round of every tournament, he made sure those basics were in order before he started his takeaway. Of course, you could try making corrections in midstream like most golfers do, but there's no need to work that hard."

Andy, trying to make sense of all this, summed it up with an analogy. "Doc, you mean it's sort of like me getting into the doghouse with my wife, and then buying her a gift to make up for what I did wrong. It'd probably be better if I just did the right thing in the first place."

"You're catching on. The 3 Fundamentals of Success are to your mental games what your grip, alignment and posture are to your physical games. The more solidly you build your starting point, the fewer corrections you'll have to make later on."

"Starting point? How to think? It almost sounds as if you want us to regress to being children," Jason said.

"Close. Although I wouldn't say it's *re*gressing. I would say it's more like *pro*gressing to a child-like state. We should always strive to use our instinctive learning ability. It's not only the fastest way to progress, it's also a skill that most adults let slip away without even realizing it."

For the next few hours the five men relaxed and talked, giving Doc a great opportunity to get to know them better. Doc asked most of the questions and listened. He learned about their goals and the reasons why they thought they weren't getting any better. He heard all of their rants and raves. He also heard a few jokes and war stories. If Doc had sat in on a full season of after-game conversations, he wouldn't have known any more about each member of this Saturday morning foursome. Someone suggested they exchange e-mail addresses and phone numbers, which they did. Upon hearing that Frank was a former teacher and well-read on the history of golf, Doc asked if he would do a little research for the group from time to time. Frank agreed. They also decided to meet every two weeks because that would give them time to digest the ideas Doc would be exposing them to. At that rate, they would finish the nine lessons just before the U.S. Amateur in late August, which Kip was gearing his competitive summer toward.

At the end of the evening, Kip summed up the mood. "Doc, I think I can say for all of us that you've really got our attention. I don't know exactly where this journey is going to take us, but it sounds pretty interesting."

"I'm glad you feel that way," Doc replied, "and I'm sure the lessons will meet your expectations. Next time we meet, we'll get started on the first lesson. It's an exciting one, because you're going to learn how to aim your arrows right at the bull's-eye."

The 1st Fundamental of Success

HOW TO THINK

CHAPTER 4

GOALS

When Kip, Jason, Andy and Frank arrived at River Bend to play golf two Saturdays later they had a problem. The heaviest fog in years had descended on the course, making it difficult to see a flagstick even 100 yards away.

"Let's wait a while for the fog to lift," urged Kip. "I wouldn't even know which way to aim if we start out in that pea soup."

"Aw come on," pressed Andy. "I'm dying to get out there and bang the ball around. Besides, fog isn't all bad. It hides my banana ball."

The men bantered back and forth until impatience ruled the day. Once they could see well enough to determine the general direction of a ball hit from the tee, they started out. However, the fog was persistent and hung around most of the morning. It wasn't until much later that they began to see more clearly.

• • •

"Here you are! I've been looking forward to seeing you again," Doc said enthusiastically the following evening. "I've put some refreshments out, so take a seat and help yourself."

"Man, did you see that fog yesterday morning?" Kip whistled. "I'm glad we don't have to play in that stuff all the time."

"Yes, it was quite something," agreed Doc. "But it brings up a good point. Since we're going to talk about goals today, I was wondering if yours are crystal clear, or if they're a little foggy like the weather was yesterday?"

"Boy, you don't beat around the bush! We've hardly settled in and you're already starting the lesson," said Kip, hurrying to pull up his chair.

"By the time some people settle in, guys, others have already walked away with the hardware," replied Doc. "You'll reap bigger rewards if you know what you want right out of the gate.[5] Last week I heard about your goals. A few of them were well thought-out, but many needed help. I also heard all about your frustrations on the golf course and how unhappy you were with your mental approach, so I'm ready to get started if you are."

To say the men were surprised at Doc's directness would be an understatement, yet at the same time, they knew they were there to learn something. Doc could see from their expressions that they were ready, so he got right to business.

"Most people see setting goals as an exercise we do with pen and paper at the kitchen table, when we finally decide we want to accomplish something. In reality, setting goals is something we do every day, all day long, with very little thought. The way you dress yourself in the morning is related to the goal of how you want to present yourself. The amount of effort you put into your job is determined by what you want to get out of your career. And of course, how much energy you put into golf is determined by what you want to achieve.

"Yet despite all of this goal-setting activity, many people, including you, realize they need clearer goals because they aren't happy with how far they've progressed. So it would make sense to be certain you're not just setting goals, but that you're setting goals properly.

"That's why today you're going to consciously learn how to set goals the proper way. That'll give you the underlying skill to set them effectively from now on, even when you aren't aware you're doing it."

"Hey, I'm all for that," Kip acknowledged, "but from my experience, setting goals is hard work. I think that's one of the reasons I haven't spent as much time on it as I should."

"No need to worry," assured Doc. "There's an easy way for you to go about it. **Your goal-setting program is made up of just three questions – why, what and who – plus four rules,** which we'll discuss as we go." Then Doc paused, and added, "Plus, you'll need to be able to climb a ladder."

"What?" asked Andy, completely confused.

"Not what, Andy, WHY?" laughed Doc. "The starting point for any achievement is Why do you do what you do? In this case, **Why do you play golf?** – although it's essentially the same question you could ask yourself no matter what you're trying to accomplish."

"Doc, are you telling me if I want to be successful in the roofing business I have to know why I'm in it?"

"It would certainly help, Andy. If Kip wants to be a successful salesman, he'll never go wrong by asking himself why he's in that field. Jason needs to know why he's a student if he's attending classes after the age of consent, and Frank should ask why he's retired if he wants to be sure of enjoying it. That being said, our situation is that we're playing golf, so our question remains Why do you play golf?"

Frank held his hand up in the form of a stop sign. "Hold on, Doc. I'd like to make some notes."

"Oh, forget the notes. Let's get going," chided Andy.

"Andy, my boy," Frank responded, "it's worth writing a few things down. There's an old Chinese proverb about learning: I hear and I forget. I see and I remember. I do and I understand. I also know from my classroom days that people always learn better when they participate, and writing is a form of participation. You do what you want, but I'd suggest making notes as we go so we don't forget the important ideas, or have to come back to them later."

"I'll take that under advisement," Andy quipped, quietly reaching for his book and a pen.

"So, Doc, can you give me a minute?" Frank asked.

"Sure, Frank," answered Doc. After a few moments, he continued. "So, Why do you play golf? Do you play for exercise or social contact? Do you play for the exhilaration of seeing the ball go where you want it to go? Maybe you want to compete, or make a living at the sport. Over time, your reasons may change. That's why it's useful, on occasion, to take a look at your underlying motivation and see if it fits with what you're doing."

After the men thought this through, Doc went on. "The good thing about completing this awareness step is that you create a starting point. You're now prepared to set goals by answering the question What? What do you want to do? What do you want to accomplish? What haven't you done yet? **What are your goals?"**

"Doc," said Jason, "I heard somewhere that we're supposed to have multiple goals. Does that mean we should have long-, medium- and short-term goals, or does it mean lots of each type?"

"Both, Jason. You should have lots of each type, as you put it, in order to reduce the possibility you'll achieve a high watermark and say, Is that all there is? **Multiple goals will keep you in motion, always looking forward to the next exciting challenge on your list.**

"As for the time frames, first you should have long-term goals for the obvious reason that they give you an overall direction and purpose. Within that framework, however, they should be the type that help you grow as a person, rather than achieve a certain public image.[6]

"Next, you need medium-term goals because they are the processes or benchmarks of improvement that connect short- and long-term goals. For example, you may have medium-term goals to improve the percentage of greens you hit, or to learn a greater variety of shots. In other words, medium-term goals are vehicles for mastering the tasks[7] of your discipline, on your way to achieving long-term success.

"Finally, you should have short-term goals[8] **because these are the ones that focus your attention right from the start.** In fact, short-term goals have more impact on actual performance and getting into the zone than long-term goals, so it's important that you take them seriously.

"A short-term goal in a round of golf might be to hit the first fairway or par the first hole. Then, as your day progresses, having other goals, such as making X number of birdies or consecutive one-putts, keeps the game interesting. Short-term goals also include ones you make up on the fly. If your first goal is to par the opening hole but something goes wrong, your ability to reset your goal is absolutely key.[9] Doing this prevents you from giving up and saying the day is lost. The reverse is just as important if everything is going well. In that case, you need to set slightly higher goals as you go to keep yourself challenged."

"Yeah, I guess that makes sense, but I'm still worried about my long-term goals, Doc," Jason confessed. "Some people have great goals and seem to be able to look way into their future, but there must be something wrong with me. I want to play on the PGA Tour and all that, but I only seem to be able to see a few years ahead. Is that okay?"

"Jason, Jack Nicklaus said that when he joined the pro tour at age 21, he only saw himself playing until about the age of 35. As we all know, he ended up playing successfully for much longer than that. He also didn't really consider trying to beat Bobby Jones's record of 13 majors until, at age 32, he had 12 of them under his belt and the press made him aware of how close he was to Jones's record. He finally won his last major at age 46, 11 years past the age he had earlier seen himself retiring.

"The point is, as time passes and your skills increase, your ability to see further and more clearly will improve. Although the purpose of goals is to cut through the fog, even on a clear day the human eye can only see so far. So for the time being, be content with how far into the distance your vision takes you, and leave it at that. There's no need to force the issue."

Doc leaned back in his chair, giving the men a chance to digest this first segment of the goal-setting process. Then, after a few moments, he resumed speaking. "Now, with your understanding of the value of multiple goals as a background, let's talk about one or two at a time, and set them properly. For this, I'd like your help, Kip. I understand from our conversation last time that you've been through a number of training courses related to your job, including some on setting goals. So, you know there are four rules to setting proper goals. What's the first one?"

"That's as easy as Sales & Management 101," Kip replied. **"The first rule of setting proper goals is that they must be specific.**[10, 11] And I think I know exactly where you're headed. In the beginning, we came to you because we wanted to improve our golf games, but I bet you didn't think that was a very specific objective, did you?"

As Doc shook his head, confirming Kip's suspicion, Frank jumped into the conversation. "How about saying we want to be more consistent? I think everyone wants that."

"On its own, consistency is not a clear goal," explained Doc. "After all, does consistent mean a spread of 10 shots from your best round to your worst, or does it mean a spread of 15 shots? Maybe consistent means avoiding mishits. And what's a mishit? You have to define the word 'consistent,' or your goal will be as hard to see as the first hole was in the fog yesterday."

"Hmmmm. I see what you mean."

"I've got it," chirped Andy. "Our goal should be to hit better shots."

"You think so, Andy? Does hitting better shots mean hitting the ball straight when you normally slice it? How straight is straight? Does it curve 10 feet or 10 yards? How often do you have to do it – 10 times in a row, or just once in 10 tries? Once again, you need to define exactly what a good shot is."

"Okay, Doc, I'll tell you what," Andy replied. "I've got this big banana ball everyone laughs at. What I'd like to do is drive the 11th green at River Bend – just once this season. It's 312 yards long and for me to hit the green, I'd have to hit the ball pretty straight. How's that?"

"Good thinking, Andy. You might be selling yourself a little short, because I think you have the potential to accomplish more than just one goal, but if you want to use it as a start, go for it."

"How about this one?" ventured Kip. "I'd like to make shooting a new personal best one of my goals."

"Now that's really hitting the nail on the head! A lot of people wouldn't choose a goal like that because they're afraid of putting themselves on the line. The value of something so specific, though, is that it funnels all your energy toward your target, instead of letting it run around haphazardly. That being said, you've got my attention, Kip. Why do you want to shoot a new personal best?" asked Doc.

Kip's answer revealed that he had thought the idea through before. "Well, when I first started playing golf, I got excited every time I shot a lower score. I remember breaking 100 for the first time, then 85 and so on, until one day I broke par, and was on cloud nine for a week. Yet for some reason, I eventually stopped trying to shoot lower scores and worked on perfecting my swing instead. I guess I thought a person could only go so low.

"Then a couple of years ago, Annika Sorenstam shot 59 in a

tournament, plodding along 'hitting fairways and greens – just fairways and greens,' as she always says. The way I heard it, Pia Nilsson, the Swedish golf coach, and her Golf 54 program put the idea of shooting in the 50s in Sorenstam's head. So I thought to myself, if one of the best golfers in the world thinks that way, maybe I should be thinking that way too. With the U.S. Amateur coming up, I figure the lower my personal best is, the better the odds are I'll shoot a good score when it really counts."

"Pretty reasonable, I'd say. What's your personal best so far?"

"It's 64, which was the River Bend course record until Robbie broke it last year. When I think about it, though, I'm not sure if I should be trying to shoot in the 50s or if I should just try to improve by one. What would you do?"

"I'd borrow a ladder from your buddy over here," Doc advised. "Andy, you use ladders to scale those roofs you work on, don't you? Do you think you could lend one to Kip here, figuratively speaking, that is?"

"Sure, buddy. Do Jason and Frank need one too? I've got a million more where those came from."

"You're too generous," chuckled Doc. "We're going to use a mental ladder to do the **Ladder Drill.** It'll help you determine how difficult you should make any goal, whether it be long-, medium- or short-term, or whether it's for accomplishing something in your personal or sporting life.

"Kip, thinking of the new personal best you'd like to shoot, write the first number that comes to your mind on the middle rung of the ladder."

Kip wrote the number down inside his book. "I'll try 63, Doc, but I'm not really sure what it should be."

"That's fine for now. I want you to test how it feels to have a target score, one harder than the one you just wrote down. So, how does 62 feel to you?"

"It feels pretty exciting, Doc, but I'm not really sure. It feels a bit unsettling at the same time."

"That's fine. Remember those feelings, and stay with me. Let's go back up the ladder. What does your original number – 63 – feel like now?"

"Mmmm," Kip said, considering the question. "Since you've moved me down and back up again, 63 doesn't really interest me anymore. If I'm going to do all the work I need to do to improve, I think I'd want a better payoff than just one stroke."

"Good. Your sense of focus is starting to kick in. Now let's sharpen it further by going the other way again. How would it feel for you to have a target score of 61?"

"61 would start to make me feel stressed."

"How about 60? What does that feel like to you?"

"Doc, that number is absolutely out of the question for me right now," answered Kip adamantly, his face straining at the thought. "Maybe someday, but it's way too hard for me to believe in yet."

"You've done a good job, Kip. **By going up and down the ladder and noticing how you react to each challenge, you'll find the goal that's right for you.** From what Robbie's told me, you have the technical ability. I can see for myself that you're keeping yourself in shape physically, and no one can question your desire. I think you're capable of shooting 62, so if you work toward it, it'll very likely happen."

"Hey, Doc. Thanks for the confidence. Yeah, I think I just might be able to handle that."

"Fantastic, Kip. Then go back to the place on the ladder where you wrote down 63, and replace it with 62. That's your new goal. The rest of **you will know you've selected the right goal when it's easy enough to feel possible, yet difficult enough to interest and excite you,**" Doc explained.

"Excuse me, Doc. I wonder if I could have another chance to set a specific goal," pleaded Frank. "I blew it the first time. What if, instead of trying to be consistent, I said I'd like to lower my handicap. It's eight now, although it was two a long time ago. If I could even get it down to six, I'd start getting excited about my game again."

"Smart choice, Frank," Doc replied. "Almost anything can be a goal, as long as you're very specific, and for the most part you'll find that anytime you translate your goal into numbers like we just did, you'll help yourself be specific."

"Doc, what about the people who say they play golf for enjoyment and don't want to get caught up in the stress of striving?" Andy questioned, not quite ready to buy in all the way. "They just want to relax. That's okay, isn't it?"

"Absolutely. Enjoying golf is a valid goal, but once again, people need to define enjoyment. Every decision bears a consequence. So, once a person says he isn't going to strive for any other goal, numerical or otherwise, he must then accept that he's not allowed to complain about his performance. In the same way, once you say your only objective is to drive the 11th green, you have no right to ever complain to anyone about the scores you shoot, or even your slice for that matter."

Andy squinted at Doc as he considered the statement. Everything Doc had said seemed to add up, so Andy wondered if he had boxed himself in with his goal. Maybe one goal *was* too limiting. Maybe he needed more, and larger, goals. Andy wasn't sure. To be truthful, he was a little worried his buddies were going to get more out of this exercise than he was. Despite that, this bout of serious thinking was uncomfortable for Andy, so he handled the situation the way he normally did. Waving his stocky arms as if he didn't care, Andy said, "Why would I complain, Doc? Driving the 11th green will put me in the hall of fame with these bandits. That's all I want."

In contrast, the logic of setting goals had hit home for Jason. "I think I've got the idea, Doc. If I qualified for the tour someday, it would be better to aim at being one of the top 10 or 20 players, let's say, than shooting for something as vague as a high-ranked player, wouldn't it?"

"Sure, Jason. However, when the day comes, how would you

even know you're a top 10 player? That might seem like an odd question, but you'll understand better when Kip gives us the second rule. Kip?"

"Okay, Doc. **The second rule of proper goal-setting is goals must be measurable.** From what I know about it, if someone wanted to be a top 10 player, he'd have to figure out how that ranking is calculated," Kip added.

"What's so hard about that?" Jason shrugged. "If I made the top 10 on the money list, I'd be a top 10 player, wouldn't I?"

"According to you," answered Doc. "But there are pros playing the PGA Tour who are in the top 10 of the world ranking, yet aren't in the top 10 of the PGA Tour money list. They would legitimately challenge you for top 10 bragging rights."

"Big deal. I'd be pretty rich no matter what list I was on. Aren't we just splitting hairs?"

Doc shook his head. "Not really. How would you like to be in the top 10 of the PGA Tour money list and not get to be one of the 10 Americans automatically eligible to play in the Ryder Cup? You might not measure up on the Ryder Cup ranking system since it's not based on the world rankings or the money list. That can happen. Depending on which top 10 list he wanted to make, a tour player would have different strategies. His selection of tournaments, how many he would play, and whether they are inside or outside of North America would be different for each goal."

"You've got me, Doc," Jason conceded. "I didn't know it was so important to decide how we want to measure our goals. And now that you say that, I don't know why I stopped doing it, but I used to record the number of greens and fairways I hit, plus my birdies and up and down percentage, so I'm thinking it would be a good idea to do that again.[12] It would be a way of measuring my progress against my goal of being the number one junior in the state, right?"

"Yes, that would be an excellent strategy, Jason, but you're not out of the woods yet. The question I'll put to you now is: Do you really think you can be number one? I'll ask Kip what rule number three is so you know where I'm headed."

Right on cue, Kip answered, **"The third rule of setting proper goals is they must be realistic."**

"So, Jason, do you have the game right now to achieve that goal?" Doc asked.

"Well no. My game isn't good enough yet, but I thought the purpose of setting a goal was to have something to work toward?"

"It is, but you have to ground yourself in reality," advised Doc. "You need to draw a line, not necessarily a solid one; it could be a dotted one between where you are and where you want to go. By that I mean you need to fill in at least some of the steps necessary if you want a goal to be realistic.

"For example, Tiger decided early in his pro career that to reach his goals, he had to fine-tune his swing and increase his strength. Jack Nicklaus decided when he first joined the tour that he needed to learn to draw the ball, as well as fade it, if he was going to be successful. Both these men were assessing the steps necessary to reach their goals.

"In your case, if your scoring average is 74 and you need an average of, let's say, 73 to be number one, what would the steps be to get there? When you create steps to bridge the gap, your goal becomes more realistic. Does that make sense to you?"

"Yeah," nodded Jason. "I've got a lot more things to consider than I thought. After we're done here I'm going to go over my game and see what I need to work on."

"Perfect! Now let's look at the fourth rule. What is it, Kip?"

"This is an easy one, Doc. **The fourth rule of proper goal-setting is goals must have a timeline.** It's probably so that we don't dream our lives away."

"Exactly. Anyone who's ever crammed for a high-school exam knows that setting a timeline is an easy way of making us focus on getting things done. So, Frank, how about adding a timeline to the goal of lowering your handicap?"

Frank pointed a finger at his own chest. "You want *me* to tell you when?" he asked "Oh. I was thinking I'd just do it sometime this summer."

Doc looked at Frank and waited patiently.

"Ha ha," Frank laughed sheepishly. "I guess if I used to make students get their assignments done by a certain date, you're not going to let me get away with that answer, are you? All right, I'll say the timeline is September 20th, the last day of summer. That makes more sense anyway. It'll get me going right now."

Thinking that Frank's answer signaled the end of the lesson, Kip pushed back his chair, stood up and generally looked like he was ready to pack it in for the evening. "This has been really good information, Doc. I bet the University of Aurora players you work with have solid goals, and that's probably one reason why they've done so well in the past few years. I'm already looking forward to coming back and learning more next time."

"Exactly where do you think you're going?" Andy taunted.

"I'm going home," Kip said, looking around at his friends' faces.

"And who do you think you're going home with?" Andy

quizzed, as he grabbed the car keys lying on the table. "It sounds like you want to go it alone."

"I don't get it. Aren't we all traveling together?"

Andy winked knowingly at Doc. "See. You didn't think I was listening, did you, but I remember you said there was one more part to setting goals, and it has something to do with Who. You can tell me about it, even if this guy here wants to start walking down the road by himself."

"Oh right!" Kip remembered, pulling up his chair and sitting down again. "Sorry, guys. I'm listening."

"You remembered correctly, Andy," Doc confirmed. "Highly successful people tend to share their journey with others. So the third question to ask yourself when setting a major goal is: **Who are you going to make the journey with?** Who are your virtual or real traveling companions?" Doc added.

"When you say traveling companion, Doc, I presume you mean someone like a teacher or a coach or mentor. Or do you mean a hero, as in a role model?" asked Frank.

"It could be any, or all, of those people. You could probably even think of a few others."

"The man up above," said Andy "I see athletes on TV all the time saying they couldn't have done it without His help. Is that what you mean?"

"Sure. That's another great example. Each of the figures you fellows mentioned is someone you can imagine helping you along the way. They don't always have to be present physically. Ben Crenshaw won the Masters in 1995 a few days after he buried Harvey Penick, his lifelong coach. Crenshaw said he played that week as if he had a 15th club in his bag. In his mind, he shared that victory with Penick."

"Doc, I'm not sure about something. Can we share our achievements with a hero we've never met?" wondered Jason. He then added hopefully, "Could Tiger Woods be my traveling companion, even if I haven't met him?"

"He could. Anyone you can hold in your mind's eye can be your companion."

Jason paused for a moment to consider how exciting that would be. "Oooh, that's cool," he said.

"Let me flesh out the concept a bit more," said Doc. "The beauty of companions,[13] virtual or otherwise, is they act as unwavering guideposts. If you know them, they can offer objective advice and support. Also, their belief in you will be steady and consistent even though yours will weaken at times. If you don't know them, you can imagine what they'd say and that advice will work just as well.

"Just remember, though, that when your companion is someone you wish to imitate, as opposed to take advice from, it's best to select someone whose ability is similar enough to yours,[14] so that the stretch is possible. For that reason you might want to imitate Tiger's fitness habits instead of his shot-making skills. A person like Kip, whose ability is closer to yours, Jason, would be a better choice. Otherwise you could become frustrated.

"In the end, when you set goals, be sure to write down who you want to make the journey with. You'll be amazed at how those people will invigorate you."

Doc then asked, "Who are the virtual or real people you're sharing your journey with now, and who would you like to have join you?"

"Well, it would certainly be easy for the four of us to travel together," decided Kip. "We play often enough that we could talk about your lessons and encourage each other to apply them properly."

"I'm with you there, Kipster," Andy chimed in. "And Doc, that was pretty simple. All we have to remember is why we want to do something, what we want to do, and who we want to do it with. You've sure got me into the idea of setting goals when I never would've done it on my own. Can you imagine me saying to my buddies, 'Come over to the house today, guys. We'll have some beer and pretzels and set some goals.' Somehow I don't think that would go over well with the crew I hang out with."

"I'm happy you enjoyed it," said Doc.

Knowing the lesson was over for sure this time, Kip got up and playfully snatched the keys back from Andy. "Well, Doc, I'm glad I stayed for the Who part," he said. "It's something I haven't paid much attention to before."

"Perfect," replied Doc. "Now you and your friends are on the right path."

CHAPTER 5

SEGMENTING

The benefit of having two weeks between sessions with Doc soon became apparent to the Saturday morning foursome. Originally they would have been happy to plow right ahead and hear all the lessons in one sitting. This way, however, they came to appreciate the value of setting goals more than if they had rushed through the lessons all at once.[15] In fact, as the weeks passed, the men noticed the same benefit after every lesson.

During this break, each of them evaluated their golf and personal goals according to the criteria Doc had outlined. For example, although Jason was a good student, like so many teenagers, he became restless sitting in a classroom day after day. After all, if he was going to become a golf pro in the long run, how long did he really need to hang in there? So he asked himself why he was going to school. His answer reconfirmed why he continued attending classes – college life would not only be a great social time for him, but college golf would be a great stepping stone to a pro career. Of course a degree would also be a valuable asset regardless of how his golf career turned out. Answering why, in his case, recommitted Jason to his next few years of education.

Kip looked into the 'what' of setting goals. As a result, in addition to his ambition to earn a spot in the Masters as an amateur, Kip's well-rounded goal-setting program now included his personal and business life. The process made him feel more balanced and confident overall.

Besides the free time to play golf, Frank had some post-retirement projects he had always wanted to start. So he began thinking about traveling companions for those projects as a way of setting them in motion.

Andy did some thinking about his goals too – just not as much as the others.

However, the more they asked themselves why, what and who questions, the more complex their goal-setting programs became. They would have to find some way of breaking down all these goals into more manageable pieces. Luckily, the lesson this week was on segmenting.

• • •

When the men arrived at Doc's house on Sunday evening, there was a magazine and a package of a dozen golf balls sitting on the patio table. Some old golf balls and a few clubs, including a driver, rested nearby as well.

"What's with the brand new balls, Doc? Are you giving out freebies today?" asked Andy.

"Oh," Doc replied, "I have a special challenge for you."

"We're ready for anything you throw at us. Bring it on."

"Well, okay. If you're ready to get down to business, here it is. If I put 12 golf balls on 12 tees and asked you to hit them, how far do you think they would go if you added up all the distances?"

"Well, it's got to be an awfully long way," declared Kip. "If a person only averaged 250 yards, let's see…the total would be almost two miles. Do you want me to give it a go?"

"Sure. Let's walk over a little closer to the riverbank, and Kip, since you're going to try, bring that driver along with you, too, would you?" After walking a short distance, Doc added, "I'll have you aim at the golf course on the other side of the river."

"Boy, looking across that river really brings back memories," Kip said, staring at the scene.

"How so?"

"Well, one day when I was a junior member at River Bend, a friend and I went to the back of the range to see if we could drive a ball across the river. At the time we were pretty young. I'm telling you, we must have hit dozens of range balls into the river before someone figured out what we were doing and sent the pro out, who hauled us back to the clubhouse by our ears. The club manager wanted to take our memberships away, but my dad got him to just suspend us for a while. I paid for it back home though. Dad was pretty upset."

"I love childhood stories, Kip. When we get done here, I'd like to hear more about that incident."

"Sure."

"Good. Now that you're older though, Kip, the river shouldn't pose too much of a problem for you, should it? I'll set these balls up for you, and let's see if you can drive them all the way across." Doc took 12 tees out of his pocket and stuck them into the ground in a cluster. With a mischievous grin, he placed the unopened box of balls on the tees which acted as a platform for the package. When he was finished, Doc folded his arms and stood back. "Two miles, Kip? I'll wager you couldn't hit them 10 feet."

"Come on, Doc. That's not fair," Kip complained. "You have to let me break them out of the box and hit one ball at a time."

Shaking his head at the trick Doc was trying to pull on him, Kip reached down, took the lid off the box and extracted a sleeve of three balls. Then he broke open that package, took one of the tees from the cluster, and teed up a single ball. With an effortless swing, Kip sent it soaring into the sky, across the river and safely onto the golf course almost 300 yards away. Kip turned to Doc, shrugged his shoulders and said, "That's more than 10 feet."

"Of course it is," admitted Doc. "If you keep hitting them one at a time, you'll probably get the two miles you said you could out of those balls. Obviously, the point I want to make with this challenge is that sometimes goals appear to be too large, or difficult to handle. On the other hand, if you break them down into small manageable segments, there's no telling how much you can accomplish. Last session you set some goals for yourself, so I want to show you a couple of techniques for breaking them into smaller portions."

As the men casually made their way toward the patio table, Doc began his explanation. **"There are two ways to segment tasks. One is to use fractions. The other is to use parts.** I'll give you an example of each to show you the difference, beginning with mini games."

"Mini games, Doc?" asked Kip, raising his eyebrows. "We play Nassau, quota-points and skins. What do you mean by mini games?"

"A mini game is a smaller version of the normal 18-hole game, or a fraction of it.[16] It could be nine holes, six holes, three, two holes or even one. It could also be one shot at a time. If one of your goals is to shoot a personal best of 6 under par, let's say, you might segment it into a series of three-hole mini games. Your objective would be to try your absolute best to play each of them in 1 under par. Once you've played them, you'd put that segment behind you, regardless of how well you did. Then you'd begin all over to play the next three-hole segment in 1 under par, and so on and so on, until the round is complete."

"Doc, what's the big deal about that?" Jason inquired. "I thought we're supposed to try our best all the time anyway? Why do we need mini-game segments?"

"Excellent question. The objectives of short-term goals – mini games in this case – are to give you feedback and success. If you see golf as a game of 18 holes, then you're only getting feedback at the end of the round, when you add up your score. Unfortunately, you would only see success and have positive feedback as often as you are satisfied with your game."

"Yeah, that happens once every blue moon," Frank said, shaking his head knowingly and pulling out a chair to sit down.

"On the other hand, if you use mini games," Doc continued, "you'll have more opportunities for positive feedback and success.[17] Three-hole mini games will give you six occasions per round. If you chose a two-hole mini game, you'll have nine occasions etc., etc. In addition, failures can be put aside faster because their impact is shorter lived, meaning that you'll progress quicker."

With all the men comfortably seated now, Jason persisted. "Gee, Doc, the pros always say they're playing one shot at a time. Isn't that the way we should be playing?"

"Yes," Doc agreed. "In the long run, you do want to play one shot at a time. But just like we saw when using the ladder drill for your personal best score last session, some goals are too difficult to take on all at once. Mini games are stepping stones toward an ultimate goal, in this case, one shot at a time. The better you get at playing them, the more comfortable you'll feel making your mini games smaller and smaller, until one day you'll actually play one shot at a time as well as a professional does.

"That being said, like any goal, the size of the mini game you choose at any particular time is important, so let me offer you this guide. **You'll know you need a larger, or smaller, mini game when you're having trouble sticking to your game plan. Conversely, you'll know you're working with the right size mini game when your attitude toward it feels patient.**

"Once you experiment with that idea a few times, you'll get the feel. I know that's a lot to think about, so would you like me to slow down, or are you ready to move on?" After a few contemplative moments, the men nodded for Doc to continue.

"Fine. With that in mind then, and thinking of the goals you set last week, let's finish up the first portion of our lesson with this question:

"What fractions could you break your goals into to make them easier to achieve?"

"Doc, not every goal we have is as easy to break up into fractions as a game of golf is. How do we segment something like improvement, or learning a new shot?" asked Frank.

"Ahhh. Another excellent question! That's why I have another example to explain how to segment a task into parts." Doc picked up the golf magazine sitting on the table and handed it to his questioner. "There's an interesting article in here. Would you do us a favor and read the section I've highlighted out loud?"

"My pleasure, Doc." Frank took the magazine, turned to the article Doc had marked and began:

"What Does It Take To Earn $1 Million Playing Golf?"

We all know professional golfers have pretty amazing skills. On Sunday afternoons, you can turn on your television to see the best of the best, at the peak of their games, pulling off clutch shots on demand. For the moment, though, forget about beating Tiger or the other top 10 money leaders. Let's say all you want to do is make a good living playing golf. If that's your objective, how many greens do you think you'd need to hit per round, to be a PGA Tour millionaire?

You might say 15, thinking the pros rarely miss a shot. Actually that's too high. Maybe you'd say 12 because you know the pros can really scramble around the greens. You'd still be too high.

According to the PGA Tour money list, last season Aaron Baddeley hit slightly fewer than 11 greens per round – 10.8 to be exact – finished 78th on the money list and earned $1,006,006.[18]

You should be encouraged. As a reader you're probably thinking there are days when the better players at your club hit that many greens. Maybe you're one of them.

Here are a few other stats readily available on the PGA Tour website – www.pgatour.com. Last year, Aaron Baddeley hit 53.3 percent of the fairways, 60.8 percent of the greens, and made 50.8 percent of his sand saves. He had 28.09 putts per round while knocking in 3.62 birdies every 18 holes.

"There's more in the article," concluded Frank, putting down the magazine, "but that's all you have highlighted."

"Thanks, Frank," said Doc. "Even though that magazine is a couple of years old, you'll find that the numbers that bring you a very handsome income are very similar for last year, or for any year on tour. The only difference is, given inflation, more and more players are becoming millionaires every season.

"The reason I wanted you to hear that story is because you might not be able to relate to the talent of a player like Aaron Baddeley as a whole. Also, we can't divide his success into fractions, but when we break it down into parts, trying to achieve similar success is more manageable. In this case, the parts are Baddeley's skills, such as ball striking, bunker play, putting, or even concentration, fitness, diet and attitude. So the second segmenting question you should ask yourself is: **What parts could you break your goals into to make them easier to achieve?**"

"Well, Doc, I already know the tour pros are better than me," Frank pointed out, "but just because I know the segments that make up their million-dollar winnings doesn't mean I can do the same thing."

"You're right about that," agreed Doc. "The point is, though, segments do tell you what you need to work on, and segmenting will help you get better. Let's say you want to improve your chipping around the green. Most people would simply go out and hit 50 or 100 shots with the hope that repetition will groove their motor skills.

"On the other hand, people who segment challenges take a different approach. They look at the parts of a technique, the chipping technique in this case, like layers of an onion. They dissect the challenge layer by layer until they find a part that's small enough for them to manage an improvement. Then they move on to the next part or layer."

Andy frowned and rubbed his eyes. "Somehow I think this is going to make me cry. How many layers can there be to chipping, Doc?"

Doc got up before answering the question. He walked past Andy on his way to selecting a pitching wedge and two balls resting beside the driver Kip had used earlier. As he did, he consoled Andy with a pat on the back. "More than there are golf balls in that package I asked Kip to hit across the river."

Doc threw the balls on the ground and chipped them to a spot about 20 yards away. "Fellows, let's say each of those two shots finishes five feet from the cup, but the first is directly behind the hole and the second is short and left. Statistically there's no difference between the two, and no way of measuring what you should have done better, even though the first is a much better shot than the second.

"However, segmenting would tell you what you need to work on. The outside layer in our onion analogy might be the line the ball starts out on. The next could be the height of the chip, then how close it came to landing on the spot you intended it to. The middle layers might be whether the ball rolls out or checks up. Then you could look at whether it comes up short or if you hit it hard enough to roll a few inches past the hole, meaning that the shot had a chance to go in. At the heart of the onion would be your emotional state. Are you hesitant, anxious, confident? Most likely the segments I just described will give you something to work on, but if they don't, break them down even more."

"Gee," Jason worried. "What if we make segments so small that they're too boring to work on?"

"That's not likely to happen, Jason. Creating smaller and smaller segments makes things more interesting in the same way that the skin on your hand appears to be more interesting when you look at it under a magnifying glass. **Ultimately, you'll know you're choosing small enough segments when you feel as if you have a legitimate chance of taking a task to the next level of improvement.**

"Doc, that's really interesting, and I follow what you're saying about segmenting when you apply it to golf," noted Kip, "but I'm still a bit fuzzy on the idea in general terms. Maybe we'd understand it better if you could give us a quick explanation of how it works in the everyday world."

Doc put aside the wedge and sat down again. "Okay. Let's consider your own profession. **Fraction segmenting** in sales would consist of breaking your annual sales targets into monthly, weekly and daily amounts. These segments are fractions because the sales goal for a month is simply $\frac{1}{12}$ of projected sales for the entire year. The goal for a week is $\frac{1}{52}$ of the sales. Your daily goal would be $\frac{1}{365}$ of the year's sales. Sales reps who might be overwhelmed by the prospect of a large annual target often feel more comfortable if they understand how much they need to sell in a smaller time frame. It ends up being a manageable number for them to focus on.

"**Part segmenting,** by contrast, would involve taking stock of all the skills you need to make those sales. When you break each one of them down, you'll find manageable areas to improve on, such as communication, organization or product knowledge. Does that make sense?"

"Yes it does," nodded Kip.

"Okay then, now that we've talked about segmenting, I'd like to hear more about that story you started to tell earlier. What happened when you were caught driving golf balls into the river?"

"Oh right. Well, I remember my father really gave it to me for hitting those range balls away, which of course weren't mine. Then after he made his point, we had to go out for something to eat because he was hungry. As we were sitting there, and I was still shaking in my boots, Dad said, 'Kip, did any of those range balls you hit make it all the way across the river?' I told him that one of them did. He winked at me and said, 'Way to go. Soon they'll all be going across.' I went from fear to joy in an instant.

"Don't ask me how they do it," continued Kip, "but parents seem to have a unique ability. On one hand they can totally disagree with something their child does, and on the other hand they can smother the child with love. It's almost as if parents put their children's good qualities into one mental drawer to admire, and the bad ones into another."

Doc immediately saw a wonderful opportunity to take the lesson of the day a step further than he had planned. "Your father sounds like a great guy, Kip. We can learn a lot from the way he treated you because your story points out a variation of segmentation called **compartmentalization. That's when a person keeps two incompatible thoughts away from each other by placing them into separate mental compartments.** The value of doing this is that it's easier to carry on with your activity when the negative thought doesn't get in the way of the positive one. For example, even though your father was angry with you, he said what he had to say, put the thought aside, and then went on being a caring father. He didn't let the negative incident interfere with his overall attitude toward you."

Andy looked down. With a quiver in his voice he said, "Gee, Doc, Kip's lucky. I wish my father had treated me that way, but I hardly knew him."

Kip knew when Andy was pulling the wool over everyone's eyes, so he played along. "Gee Andy, it wasn't so bad down at the orphanage was it? They might not have taught you how to dress or take care of yourself but there must have been enough to eat, judging by the size you got to be."

"Yeah, I guess where there's bad there's good after all," quipped Andy, patting his stomach.

"You fellows might be kidding each other," Doc chuckled, "but the way a parent compartmentalizes is something you can apply to your golf game.

"If you have a very bad hole sometime you may feel like giving up. Despite that feeling, the best way to handle the situation is to compartmentalize it. Put the bad experience away in one drawer, the way Kip said parents do, and choose another drawer full of good experiences. The best thinkers would say 'the hole I just played may have been a disaster, but the hole I'm about to play is an opportunity.' People who are unable to use this skill say self-defeating things like 'here we go again' or 'I just can't seem to get anything going.'

"So, if you want to treat yourself as kindly as your parents would, try compartmentalizing the next time you experience a setback. You'll love the results. In fact, it's the perfect thought to leave you with before our next lesson – about self-image."

"See, Andy!" Kip said, resting his hand kindly on Andy's shoulder. "There's even hope for a sad sack like you. When Doc talks about self-image, he'll show you how to heal those emotional scars and finally make something of yourself."

Kip's verbal sparring only served to prompt a comeback from Andy. Adopting a haughty air, he replied, "Kip, it's unusual for you to be so nasty to me, but I can compartmentalize with the best. I'll choose to forget this brief lapse in your behavior by putting aside that comment and calling on the part of my brain that remembers you as the fine gentleman you normally are."

"Well, fellows," Doc said in response to this banter, "I may be giving you these lessons for free, but I'd actually pay just for the fun of being around you. Who's selling tickets to the next session?"

CHAPTER 6

SELF-IMAGE

"Hey there, Kipster, we missed you yesterday. How'd it go at the Willow Park Invitation?" asked Frank as the men gathered two weeks later for the drive over to Doc's house.

"I'm still recovering," said Kip, visibly frustrated. "I pulled a Van de Velde."[19]

"Uh-oh. Sounds like you made a big number with the lead going down the stretch."

"Hmmph. I was rolling along just great and made double-bogey on my second-last hole, to lose by one. I'm so #%*&! mad I'd sell my clubs for a buck. I hope Doc's lesson about self-image today is good, because my self-esteem needs an overhaul."

Frank was about to relate a story that Kip's comment made him think of but Jason and Andy turned the conversation to other things. Distracted, Frank forgot what he had intended to say until later.

After the men arrived at Doc's house and were settling in, Frank said, "We've got a wounded soldier for you to deal with today, Doc. The Kipster was shot down in battle and he's on life support. But before you get into rebuilding his self-image, I've just got to tell you guys about a TV show I saw this week on the same subject. I was flipping channels and caught one of those reality shows. It was about people having cosmetic surgery and getting their teeth fixed and so on. You know the type of show I mean. Well, you wouldn't believe this one woman. Even though she was pretty good-looking, she was unhappy with her nose because it was a little crooked. For my money I would have left it alone, but she went and had corrective surgery and came out looking fabulous. Then you know what she did? She turned to the doctor, looked him square in the eye and said, 'My nose is the same as it was before.' I almost fell off my chair. In fact, on the show, the plastic surgeon brought in her family and friends, and they all said she looked great, yet this woman insisted nothing had really changed. She didn't feel any better about herself either, which was the real reason for the surgery in the first place. In the end, the best they could get out of her was, 'Well, I can see you've done something, but I still look the same.'"[20]

"I can tell you one thing," Andy declared. "If I looked in the mirror every day and saw my beak pointing at my right ear, I'd sure notice if someone rearranged it so it pointed straight ahead."

Doc had been listening carefully to this and shifted forward in his chair. "You might be surprised, fellows," he said. "The same kind of thing happens to a lot of people. Most people don't realize that when they learn something new they need to make an adjustment, just like that lady needed to. Improving your posture or learning how to hit a flop shot is similar to corrective surgery. Unless you also change the way you see or feel about yourself, your scores won't improve any more than that woman's self-perception did."

Kip could see Doc meant that a person's self-image is pretty difficult to alter. "So, Doc, what does a person have to do to make the change work and build a strong self-image?" he asked.

"There are a few ways to do it," said Doc. "In fact, there are three simple techniques to use. We'll call them **Learn the Lesson, Climb the Ladder and Take the Walk.** But before we discuss them, will you fill me in on why Frank called you a wounded soldier earlier?"

After Kip repeated the painful story of his tournament loss blow by blow, Doc unexpectedly reached across the table to shake Kip's hand. "Congratulations, young man. Congratulations for working hard enough to get yourself into that situation. Congratulations for feeling some emotion instead of saying 'it just happened.' That's a cop-out. And congratulations for making the same kind of mistake two of the greatest golfers of all time made."

"Excuse me?" Kip sputtered.

"Let me explain. In the 1960 U.S. Open, Jack Nicklaus was leading by one shot when he three-putted from 12 feet on the 13th hole of the final round and lost by two. In 1961, Arnold Palmer needed only a par on the very last hole from the middle of the fairway to win his second straight Masters. He made double-bogey to lose the tournament. What you did wasn't any more of a disaster, so you're in good company.

"I realize you're feeling disappointed," Doc continued. "That's understandable. But *all* people, including every great achiever, have had similar experiences. It's how great achievers have dealt with those experiences that separates them from the average person. Once I tell you what they did, you'll almost relish your mistakes."

"I know you've got some pretty good ideas, Doc, but I'm not sure I'd go that far. Anyway, I'm all ears."

"Good. Let's go back to the classic cases of Palmer and Nicklaus. After Palmer got ahead of himself and lost the 1961 Masters, he went on to write something interesting in one of his books. To paraphrase, he brooded about it all that winter and developed a philosophy to prevent it from happening again. He resolved he would never get ahead of himself and ignore the job at hand until the ball is in the hole and the scorecards are signed.[21] Simply put, Palmer's lesson is that the game isn't over until it's over.

"Nicklaus had a similar response to his setback in the 1960 U.S. Open. If he had taken his defeat the wrong way, it might have really hurt him, because you have to remember, he was only 20 years old at the time. Fortunately, he was a skilled enough thinker to take advantage of the situation, and later wrote that he learned three lessons." Doc ticked off the points on his fingers: "Know the rules; if in doubt, ask; and repair ball marks as you'd like others to repair them for you.[22]

"The magic of their approach is that Palmer and Nicklaus improved their self-image even when they had setbacks. Not many people have that ability." Doc became more deliberate and chose his words very carefully as he explained the concept.

"By choosing to learn a lesson after a disappointment instead of assigning a label, such as unsuccessful, to themselves they came to believe that something good had come from their adversity.[23] It's a neat twist that allowed them to see every single experience, positive or negative, as one that improved their game. That concept is comforting, and if you've followed their careers, you'll have noticed they used the same technique over and over again.[24]

"In modern times Tiger has done the very same thing. During

his relative dry spell in 2002 and 2003, when he was rebuilding his swing and *only* won one major, the press kept asking Tiger what was wrong with his game. Journalists were trying to pin a label on him, but they were always unsuccessful.

"That's because Tiger simply refused the label. Instead, he told everyone that he was learning how to swing the club better. He saw himself traveling on a path to success even when the victories weren't piling up."

Kip had lived through the Tiger episode so he remembered it, but Nicklaus's feats were before his time. "Doc, are you telling us that Jack Nicklaus, a man who won 18 professional majors and two U.S. Amateur titles, couldn't find anything better to learn from a defeat than to fix a ball mark properly? Surely he could have come up with something a lot more profound than that."

"Kip," replied Doc, "with respect to this technique, there's no need to be as profound as the world's greatest philosopher. **The objective is to simply point your thinking in the right direction. Any small lesson will do the trick.** Furthermore, if you choose to focus on small lessons you'll never run out of things to learn. If, however, you look for some universal point of wisdom, you'll find yourself trying to top each lesson with one more profound than the last. That'll lead to frustration, and you'll never develop an effective way to deal with adversity."

"Hmmm, I see," said Kip. "But another thing, Doc. Why did you say a couple of minutes ago it would be a cop-out to say 'it just happened'? I thought it would be a good idea to consider a failure as 'just one of those things' and block it out."

Tapping his forehead with a finger, Doc replied, "Smart people think differently, Kip. Consider the opportunity to improve that

Palmer and Nicklaus would have lost had they been in the habit of saying 'it just happened!' They would have never learned those valuable lessons and improved their self-image.

"You have an opportunity to learn as much from your adversity as they did from theirs. What's more, I'm going to prove that you already have the built-in success mechanism Nicklaus and Palmer used. Try thinking back, and answer the following question: **What past adverse situation in your personal or professional life did you learn from, and what action did you take as a result?"**

After giving him a minute to think it over, Doc asked, "What did you come up with, Kip?"

"Well, I can think of a few situations, but there's one in particular that really hurt my pocketbook. When I first started selling, I went to see a customer with the intent of writing up a long-term contract. I got so wrapped up in what I wanted to sell him that I didn't listen to a word about his needs. Not only did I lose the sale, I lost some of my company's existing business with him because he lost confidence in us. It wasn't pretty. When I realized what I had done wrong, I decided I would always listen to people before I offered a solution. I've never made that mistake again!"

"And that's why you're a successful salesman today," Doc explained. "It's interesting to note that you didn't go home with your tail between your legs, and say, 'I'll never be a salesman.' Instead, you decided to learn a simple lesson – be a good listener – which keeps you growing. That's very different than assigning a value to your behavior, which halts your growth, not to mention that it hurts your self-image.

"All of you will have similar stories if you think about it long enough. Knowing you learned something from a negative experi-ence or setback proves you have one of the skills needed to build a successful self-image the way the great champions did. Now, let's begin to transfer your newfound talent to the golf course by working through the following: **What intense situation on the golf course have you faced that didn't turn out the way you would have liked it to?**

"And of course, the question that follows is: **What lesson can you learn from it?** Remember, fellows, the lesson you learn only needs to be a very small one."

Frank threw down his pen after making his notes. "You know, Doc, this really hits home. Last year I got penalized in a tourna-ment for having too many clubs in my bag. It irritated me and I resigned myself to the idea that I'm getting more and more for-getful as I get older. But you proved I can choose to think differ-ently. So just now I wrote down that the lesson I should have learned is to always count the number of clubs in my bag before teeing off.[25] I know that's nothing earth-shattering, but it feels refreshing to think that way. Instead of seeing myself as some worn-out relic, I see myself as a wily veteran. This idea of learn-ing the lesson steers me in the right direction, instead of allowing me to peddle in reverse like I've been doing for so many years."

"I couldn't have explained the effect any better myself. So, so much for today's first technique," said Doc, clapping his hands together in summation. "I think you're ready for the next step.

"The second technique you can use to build your self-image is called Climb the Ladder. To help us with our lesson in this fine art, let's bring in our resident expert in the field. Andy, just how does a professional climb a ladder?"

Andy was confused about what Doc's question and self-image had to do with each other, but he knew how to climb ladders and, of course, he always enjoyed being center stage. "The proper way to climb a ladder, boys, is to always look one rung above the one you're gripping. The people who get stuck are the dummies who look down or straight across. They freeze. I actually had to bring in a hydraulic bucket to rescue a University of Aurora student I hired last summer. He got way up on a ladder and was scared so stiff he couldn't move. But if he would've just kept looking up at the next rung, he could've kept on going."

"That's a pretty transparent analogy, Doc," Frank concluded. **"If we want to avoid getting stuck on a certain self-image, we have to have a mental picture of the next level we want to get to, rather than defining ourselves by where we are."**

"Exactly," replied Doc, "and that way your self-image is always improving. Let's say, for instance, that you don't have a very good up and down percentage – maybe you only have a 35 percent conversion rate. Instead of saying, 'I'm not very good at that part of the game,' you would set a target to move yourself along. What do you think the new target should be, Jason?"

"How about 50 percent? That would improve your score," Jason suggested.

"Maybe," cautioned Doc, "but it would be a better idea to go up the ladder a rung at a time, just like you did when you first used the ladder drill. You may find that 50 percent is unrealistic in the short term. As we learned before, the goal you set should be enough of a stretch that it excites you, yet not so difficult that you can't achieve it. For that reason, starting with a goal of, let's say, 40, or 43 percent, or whatever, should get you moving enthusiastically."

"Doc, do professional athletes actually do this?" asked Jason.

"They do. That's how they get to be professionals. Tiger Woods's approach to golf is a perfect example of climbing one rung at a time. When he joined the tour in 1996, everyone knew he had great potential, but he's done a lot of small things since then besides refining his swing. Tiger was a relatively skinny kid when the public first noticed him. Although he had always been into physical fitness, he refined his workouts to include stretching and aerobics. But it wasn't just for a month or two. His exercise program became a lifestyle. The sculpted physique you see on Tiger now didn't happen all in one day.

"Of course, he didn't stop with physical improvement. Tiger has continued to develop different shots for himself. We now have the term Stinger for a particular tee shot he's brought to the golf world. In addition, although not entirely new, more people are trying the metal wood chip shot from the fringe that Tiger uses occasionally.

"Tiger even went on to make fine adjustments to his diet.[26] When you add it all up, Tiger has raised himself higher and higher by simply climbing one rung after another, and although he's made a lot of progress in just a few short years, it's never over for him. People like Tiger never arrive. They're constantly in motion. You'll have success, too, if you can keep your eye on the next rung on the ladder. So, a good question to ask yourself is: **What's the next rung on the ladder for me?** Can you fellows see how that'll get you moving forward?"

"Yeah, I do, Doc," Kip said. "I just want to write down the answer to that question, if you can give me a minute…There… Okay. So what's the other technique you mentioned for building our self-image?"

"The third technique is Take the Walk, which is a visualization technique for your self-image."

"I can tell you something about taking a walk," interrupted Andy. "The other day I was in an architect's office who was doing some plans for a builder I'm working with, and these guys showed me a new building they're designing. Before it's even built, they can walk customers through it on a software program. They told me that because of it, their projects run a lot smoother and they save hundreds of thousands of dollars every year. I guess they get this advanced look at their building projects and take care of mistakes before they happen. So, have you got something like that up your sleeve for us, Doc?" Andy asked.

"I do, Andy. The walk-through I want you to take is also a way to prevent a lot of mistakes before they happen, plus build a better self-image at the same time."

"When are we supposed to do this walk-through thing, Doc?"

"You should do it before an activity, and also after it. Before a round of golf, take a mental walk through the course to plan your strategy for the day. It'll help create an image of the way you want things to turn out.[27]

"On the flip side, the walk you take after an activity has a different effect. After a round of golf, pat yourself on the back for the things you did well, and then, in a short internal conversation, mentally correct the mistakes you made. Our minds don't always know the difference between our real experiences and the fiction we can conjure up.[28] That's where the expression 'perception is reality' comes from. By correcting mistakes mentally, either in advance or after the fact, you'll start to develop the self-image of a good performer, and the confidence to handle other difficult situations whenever they might arise."

"Doc, it seems like all of these walks we take are in our minds. I guess there's an endless number of them, right?" asked Kip.

"The number certainly is endless, although you can also take physical walks that will affect your self-image. If you've ever given a public speech, you know that it's a good idea to walk into the room before the presentation. Check out the lights and audio-visual equipment. Then step to the podium and imagine you're already speaking to the audience. That trick will do wonders for making you feel comfortable when the real moment arrives. So, having said that, how do you think you could apply the same idea to golf?"

This wasn't such a tough question, although it was obvious from the men's faces that they didn't have a ready answer. For his part, Doc enjoyed the pregnant pause. It made the men think.

"I know," Kip announced eventually. "When I go to my next tournament site, I'm going to find out where they hold the presentation ceremony. Then I'm going to walk up to the spot where the winner receives his trophy and imagine everyone applauding me."

"There you go. That's a perfect example of Taking the Walk," said Doc. "And Kip, now that you've worked through this lesson, how do you see the events of your last tournament?"

"I feel a lot more comfortable now, Doc," Kip asserted. "While we were talking, I walked through it a couple of times in my mind, imagining the way I wanted it to turn out. You know what else? It just dawned on me that a person doesn't magically own a good self-image like Tiger or Vijay Singh do. It must be something you add to and create for the rest of your life, based on how you interpret your experiences."

Frank got up and took a few steps away from the table with a deliberate swagger. "Hey there, Kipster, now that you can walk the walk, it'll be easier for you to talk the talk." Then, suddenly hit by another thought, Frank turned around again. "Whoa! Just a minute here, Doc. Speaking of talking the talk, shouldn't our mental lessons have something to do with self-talk? When are we going to get to that part?"

"I've been waiting for that question," replied Doc. "I told you there would come a time when you'd ask the right question and that's the very one. Until now, we've discussed The 1st Fundamental of Success – How To Think. We've looked at how to think about your goals, and how you should break them down into manageable portions. Then we discussed how you should think about yourself.

"Since a person should think before they speak, you're now ready for The 2nd Fundamental of Success – How To Talk. It's the language of success."

The 2nd Fundamental of Success

HOW TO TALK

—— ● ——

CHAPTER 7

SELF-TALK

At the end of their last lesson, the Saturday morning foursome had been quite intrigued that Doc called self-talk the language of success. Jason was especially eager to learn how to develop his self-talk skills and said he would be willing to record his self-talk over the next two-week period, if Doc would review his notes at the next session. Jason wanted to write down whatever he said to himself when he hit good shots or bad ones, when he faced difficult situations or when someone asked how he was playing. He even promised to record what he said on the practice range. Doc said the exercise would be a valuable one, so Kip and Frank decided to do it too. As might be expected, it took a little arm-twisting to get Andy to go along, but in the end he agreed.

As a result, Doc now had four pages of written thoughts in his hands and was reading excerpts from them out loud. "'What the #@%! is the matter with me today? My game? You don't want to know.' Hmmm, sounds like someone was unhappy for a while," Doc commented, and resumed reading further down the page. "'Oh for cripes sake, could I just hit it on the green for once? Here we go again.' Sure. This seems like a pretty good cross section of things many people say on the course. 'If I could just run it up that gap, I'd catch the front of the green. Oh, I had a feeling that one was going in.'" Doc finished reading and put the papers down. "Well, at least the last little bit was positive. So, fellows, what did you learn from that exercise?"

"I can tell you, Doc," Frank replied. "There's more action going on in my head than there is down at the local zoo. I noticed some of my self-talk was good, some was terrible, and some didn't mean much at all. What I learned is that I should really be talking more positively and pumping myself up more often. That would be proper self-talk, wouldn't it, Doc?"

"That's the popular notion, Frank, but I'd like you to know a little more about self-talk than that. Besides, you'd soon grow tired of listening to yourself if pumping yourself up was all you ever did. So, our lesson today is about noticing how **our choice of words either directs our thinking away from our goals or toward them.** In order to understand how this happens, we need to look at the difference between statements, which tend to push us, and questions, which tend to pull us. We'll see that both can be positive, both can be negative, and in some cases, both can be downright ambiguous.

"For the sake of an example, imagine you're on the tee at a par 3. You've just made a swing and watched your ball land smack in the middle of the water guarding the green. Tell me anything that comes to mind."

The four men fired off comments they had made or heard in the past. Doc wrote them down, then quickly numbered each one so he could show the progression of self-talk from poor to good to better and then to best. With that done, he looked up from his notes and began to discuss what he had recorded. "The first one you came up with was **a question that elicits a negative response:** 'Why did I hit that ball in the water?' By the way, fellows, did you know that questions have the ability to Googlize your mind?"

"Googlize, Doc? As in Google, the search engine?" asked Andy.

"Right. Questions turn your mind into a search engine. If you ask Google where to buy red cars, it will set out on a search without questioning your intent, then come back with a long list of answers for you. Similarly, when you pose a question, your mind very dutifully goes out and searches for all the answers it can find. It doesn't know, or even care, why you asked. It just wants to please its master, so it piles up answer after answer until you ask it to do something else.

"When you pose a negative question, such as Why did I hit that ball in the water?, the same process is at work. In a very short time, your subconscious will have retrieved a multitude of reasons to explain why you hit the ball there. The overwhelming majority of them are detrimental to a belief in your ability. In the end, based on the balance of information you requested, the only logical conclusion to be drawn is that you're a completely incompetent golfer. That's why a negative question is the most destructive of all the varieties of self-talk. Later we'll see how you can use your Googlized mind to your advantage, but for now, I think you can see why you want to stay away from negative questions."

Andy looked at Doc and laughed. "You're no fun, Doc. I've been asking myself stupid questions like that forever. Now you don't want me to do it anymore. I hope you don't tell me the next saying we gave you is just as dumb?"

"I'm afraid it is," said Doc, "It's **a negative statement,** featuring a special culprit – the word 'don't,' as in 'Don't go there.' Speaking of which, Andy, remember that story you told us about rescuing a worker off a ladder with a hydraulic bucket? You said he was stuck. What were people telling him at the time?"

"Oh, that guy! Well, when I arrived at the scene, the rescue crew were all yelling at him 'Don't look down! Don't look down!' But of course, the more they said that, the more he looked down, and the more scared he got.

"When they brought him down he was shaking like a leaf. We were going to take him to a doctor but he said it was all in his head and he knew of a friend who could help him. But that's a story for another time. Why do you ask?"

"What I'm trying to show you, Andy, is that the mind tends not to hear the word 'don't.' Most often it hears the action words of the sentence being spoken instead, which in that situation were 'look down.' This is especially likely to happen under stress, with the result that we bring into focus the very thing we're trying to avoid. It would have been better to start off the guy on the ladder with the proper instructions in the first place. Although this idea doesn't hold water 100 percent of the time, it plays out often enough that you want to avoid the word 'don't.' We should always give ourselves and others a positive option with our first instruction."

Andy grimaced and shook his head. "I wish I'd have had you along the other day, Doc. I actually came close to driving the 11th green for the very first time, and was feeling pretty good about my swing. Then I got up to the 12th tee and said to myself, 'Okay, numskull, don't lose it!' According to what you just explained, I guess I'm a bit of an idiot for saying it that way."

"There you go again, Andy, another negative statement. In this case, **a negative affirmation.** I've written down 'You idiot' and 'You dummy' or 'You #@%!' But they're all the same."

"I don't know which way to turn, Doc. You're twisting everything I say," Andy replied half-jokingly.

Doc was starting to have a bit of fun now. He enjoyed using Andy's comments to explain the progression of statements and questions and, unwittingly, Andy was following right along. "'I don't know which way to turn' would be **an ambiguous statement,** Andy, as if our golfer had said, 'that's interesting.' The mind wouldn't know what to make of it, though at least the statement isn't completely negative."

"So what should I say then?" Andy asked, clearly frustrated.

"That's up to you, Andy, but for my purposes, you just asked **an ambiguous question.** The brain will go out and search for answers, some of which will be helpful, and some of which will be harmful. Our golfer would have asked, 'So what do I do now?' That question can elicit positive responses or, unfortunately, negative ones. You shouldn't take that chance."

"Get me outta here, Doc," Andy blurted, throwing his hands in the air. "Pick on someone else."

Doc quickly stretched out his arm in front of Andy. "Stop right there. That's **a positive statement** very similar to 'Just hit it on the green.' It has value, but it wouldn't be a bad idea if the instruction was more specific. You want to be out of here, but exactly where do you want to go? A person might want to hit the ball on the green, yet it would be helpful to let the mind and body know how to achieve the objective. Interestingly, when you direct a positive statement toward yourself as a form of encouragement, you're using a slight variation of a positive statement called **a positive affirmation.** 'You can do it,' as opposed to 'Pick on someone else,' is such an example. And despite the minor shortcomings of the former, positive statements and affirmations are the first in a series of self-talk skills that will move you forward instead of backward.

"Often you'll hear winning athletes in post-game interviews use some version of a positive statement that helped them block out stress or anxiety going down the stretch. 'Hang in there' or 'You can pull this off' are examples. So having a full complement of positive statements and affirmations to draw on is a great asset. That being said, another extremely important skill to have at your disposal is the ability to ask a positive question."

Having been in the hot seat for so long, Andy was looking for a way out. Raising his arms in surrender, he pleaded, "Doc, what do I have to do to get into your good books again?"

"Ahhh, very good," Doc replied. "That's **a question that elicits a positive response,** similar to our golf equivalent: 'What do I have to do to hit the next shot on the green?' It's a beautiful question. Your mind will go out and search for helpful answers, giving you a fighting chance of pulling off the results you want. It's an essential everyday skill, but especially useful when you're trying to make a decision and need to sort through conflicting thoughts."

"Thanks, Doc. I'm glad you taught me all this," answered Andy, looking weary from their verbal exchange. "But from now on, could you use the Kipster here instead of me to demonstrate how self-talk works? I'm bushed."

Doc was really amused now. "Are you sure we didn't rehearse this, Andy? By asking if Kip could take your place, you've just used the first of two advanced self-talk techniques. This one is called **role model substitution**. The question I had written down was: If Fred Couples was hitting this one for me, what would the shot look like? Sometimes when you just don't have anything going for you and all seems hopelessly lost, it's all right to let go of your energy completely. You then replace it with energy from someone you admire. Some people look for spiritual intervention. Other people think of a companion or role model. For fun, you should have a favorite golfer in mind whom you can call on to hit a shot for you once in a while."

Andy suddenly perked up. "Hey, I know. I could use Mark Calcavecchia because I'm sort of built like him, and he likes to cut his shots too. I'd sit right back and have the big guy hit a few shots for me when I need help. Man, that would be a big relief!" Andy turned to Kip and added a comment so quietly that not everyone heard him. "Then we'd go for a beer – just me and the Calc, you know – and talk about finesse shots."

"Beautiful, Andy! Now you're using the second advanced technique – **positive mood words.** Our golfer on the par 3 might have said, 'What club should I select if I want to make a nice, patient swing?' Your words 'big relief' are just as good, and both phrases add feeling, or a mood if you will, to the situation."

"Doc," Andy chirped, "the muttering I do from now on will never be the same. All the animals in my zoo better listen up. There's a new trainer in town."

"Great, Andy. Way to go."

"Whew, Doc," Kip sighed. "That's quite a progression you took us through. I didn't know there were so many varieties of self-talk. Pretty interesting, but does our self-talk only have an effect when we're talking to ourselves?"

"Oh, absolutely not," Doc replied. "Here's a scene you've probably witnessed before. You're walking from the parking lot to the clubhouse and a friend going the other way says, 'Hi, Kip. How's the game?' How do you normally reply?"

"Most of the time I just say, 'Aw, it's not bad,' because I've heard other people say 'Just rotten,' and I think that's kind of negative."

"That's understandable. Out of a sense of modesty, many people say the same thing you do when they're playing really well. But my question to you is: Who is listening to the answer?"

"Well, my friend asked the question, Doc. It must be him."

Doc waved his hand dismissively. "Let me tell you something, Kip," he advised. "As much as anyone might be a friend to you, when they go to bed at night and pull up the covers, the last thing they're thinking about is *your* golf game. They're thinking about their own lives. That conversation in the parking lot is rarely more than a social nicety on your friend's part, while for you it's an instruction to your rabbit-eared self-image. The answer you give will live on in your mind forever, so make it a good one."

"Doc," said Kip, trying to recover as quickly as possible, "could I say 'I'm working at it,' or, 'It's getting better all the time'?"

"Sure. Those are both excellent because they convey the idea that you are in motion, like Tiger always is. Add a smile or a wink, and you'll create a mood that'll do wonders for you."

The Saturday morning foursome was very impressed with what they had learned in this session. Now equipped with a wider and more meaningful vocabulary of terms for self-talk than simply positive or negative, they understood how even the slightest rephrasing of words could alter their focus.

"Doc, it seems from the examples you gave us that statements might be useful once in a while, but questions are the real stars of self-talk. Would that be right?" asked Jason.

"Yes it is," replied Doc. "People who ask better questions get better answers, and if you think about it, some of the greatest people in the world became famous for the questions they asked."

Doc then turned to Frank, who was busy writing in his book. "Frank, you were doing double duty this week with some research about a famous person who asked a great question. Can you tell us what you found?"

"Sure," said Frank. Putting down his pen, he retrieved some notes from the back of his book. "I came up with a pretty interesting story, if I do say so myself. I read that one day back in May of 1905, a young scientist spent an evening at a friend's house discussing physics. A few hours later, he took a ride home, still thinking about the issues he and his friend had been trying to solve. Albert asked himself, 'What would happen if the streetcar I'm riding suddenly raced away from that clock tower over there at the speed of light?' And that very innocent-sounding question helped Albert Einstein develop the theory of relativity."

"That's pretty interesting, Frank," Doc agreed. "I hadn't heard the story quite that way before." Then, addressing all of the men, Doc offered a few thoughts for them to consider. "Fellows, wouldn't it have been unfortunate if Einstein had asked himself a negative question the way so many golfers do? What if he had asked, 'Why can't I seem to make any headway on this issue?' His brain would have searched for the answers, most of which would have diverted him from a solution to his problem and attempted to explain why he was a bad physicist instead. Who knows what effect that might have had on the quality of his work and his contribution to the world of physics?

"Or, how about this? Jack Nicklaus had a habit of repeatedly asking himself two questions. They were: How am I going to win this tournament? and How do I want to play this shot? Fairly innocent questions, but just think, if Nicklaus had been in the habit of asking two different questions: Why is winning tournaments such a struggle? and Why is my bad shot an over-the-top pull?, we might never have heard of the man who was voted the greatest golfer of the 20th century."

Doc's examples provoked some thought among the group. The men began to wonder what kind of valuable, innocent thoughts they might have bottled up inside. Jason finally said, "Hey, Doc, maybe we've all got some really good questions deep down that we're not asking. Is that possible?"

Surprisingly, Doc disagreed with the possibility. "No. It's not a possibility. It's not even a probability. It's a certainty! In fact, no one knows how much potential you really have, so it would be a good idea to ask yourself this: **What great question lies inside of me, just waiting to be asked?**"

The men took a few moments to consider this, but the moments stretched into minutes. They looked like they were asking themselves great questions and then imagining how famous they would become. After a while, Doc realized he needed to get their attention. "Hey, Frank, are you there? Frank? You look like you're off in never-never land," Doc laughed, as he waved his hand in front of Frank's face.

"Mmmm, oh yeah. I'm here," Frank confirmed. "Just dreaming. You know, you really have a way of asking questions that take us for a ride, don't you, Doc? Going back to our lesson though, you've given our zookeeper some good training today, but how did we get from self-talk to questions?"

"Self-talk is what we say to ourselves, and it just happens that questions are the most powerful phrases we know how to use," Doc replied. "In fast-action sports like basketball or football, a player often doesn't have time to think a question through during the action, so he's more likely to use positive affirmations than questions. In golf, there's a lot of free time between shots, so there's an opportunity to use questions more often."

"Okay, I guess that makes sense, as usual, but another thing. Did I hear you say we should use mood words in our self-talk?"

"You sure did, and that's where there's a lot of room for improvement. **Mood words add texture to your activities, making it easier to either remember them or project the outcome you want.** Here's a brief example: Instead of saying blandly to yourself, 'I'm going to hit this ball on the green,' you could say, 'Wouldn't this ball be delighted if it parachuted to safety right beside the flagstick?' Both 'delighted' and 'safety' are mood words and can completely change how you feel about whatever you might be trying to accomplish.

"However, moods aren't just created by words. They're also created by the way you speak with your body, which leads us to what we're going to discuss next time – body-talk. Did you ever think about how your body talks?"

"Did I ever think about how my body talks?" Frank repeated slowly, scratching the back of his head. "Wow. I'm telling you, Doc, you've got more questions than there are stars in the sky."[29]

"I'll take that as a compliment, Frank, if that's all right with you. And when we meet again, we'll discuss the second of the How To Talk lessons, body-talk."

Doc got up and took a long stretch. "Ohhhhhhhhh, that feels good." Then he said, "I know it's been a full evening fellows, but the best way for us to prepare for our next meeting is for me to give you some instructions now. How about if we take a short break and go back at it for a few more minutes?"

Everyone agreed. As always, there was at least one driver and a few old golf balls located somewhere around Doc's backyard. So it didn't take long for the men to locate them and have some fun hitting a few balls across the river, as Kip had done some weeks earlier. After just a few swings they had loosened up and were ready to sit down again.

"Okay, guys. Here's the job I have for you," said Doc. "The last two weeks you kept notes for yourself on self-talk. Now I'd like you to do something similar for body-talk. Between now and the next time we meet, observe how you move your body, both on and off the course, and see if you can detect a relationship between your emotions and your motions. Your observations will help you answer a different question. In this case the question is: **What emotions do your motions create?**

"This exercise should prove to be especially informative for Kip, who has a pretty important qualifying tournament coming up. I'd like him to pay special attention to his body motions during that tournament and share what he learns with us when we meet again. As for you, Jason, you said you'll be caddying for Kip, so your job's a little different."

Doc then asked the other men to excuse him and Jason for a moment while he gave Jason a special assignment. Kip, Andy and Frank were all too happy to go back to the edge of Doc's property and hit a few more balls. Once they were out of earshot, Doc turned to Jason and said, "This is what I want you to do...."

CHAPTER 8

BODY-TALK

The next tournament on Kip's summer schedule was a critical one in his quest to compete for the U.S. Amateur title. And, as he got ready for his tee-off time in the one-day qualifier, Kip could feel the pressure building.

"Jason, I appreciate you caddying for me," Kip said anxiously. "Having a friend around should help settle the nerves a bit, but man, am I wired!"

"I'm excited too, Kip, but no problem. You'll be fine. Two under, over 36 holes at this site should earn you a spot in the Amateur, and that's a no-brainer the way you've been playing. Just go out and do it."

"You're probably right, so why am I so nervous?" Catching himself, Kip laughed. "I mean, how can I make this nervousness work for me, right?" Kip's subconscious provided an answer to this question as quickly as it forgot the previous one. "*I know. Take a deep breath...in...out.... Whewwwwww. Okay, that's better.*"

"On the tee from the River Bend Golf Club, Kip Raston," called the starter for the sectional qualifier of the U.S. Amateur.

Less nervous now, though keyed up just the same, Kip's internal monologue continued. *"This is it, Kip. You might as well act like you're going to play well. Step up there like you belong."* Kip walked confidently to the tee, located his target in the fairway, and with a perfect routine, striped a drive down the middle. The game was on.

• • •

"It sounds like you had a great day," Doc noted on Sunday night after Kip skimmed over the results of Friday's qualifier. "Let's go back over it again. I want to hear all the details. First, though, I have to tell you that taking a deep breath like you did before the opening swing was a smart thing to do. When you're nervous, a good deep breath allows you to calm down and focus on your task. Yet, despite its advantages, proper breathing is one of the least practiced skills by athletes."

"I bet I know the reason, Doc," Kip chuckled. "Breathing is so automatic, instructions aren't normally needed on the package. But you know, there must be something to this breathing idea. I have a friend who takes yoga classes and they teach him special breathing exercises. I also know most professional sports trainers encourage deep breathing and so does anyone teaching relaxation. What I'd like to know is which method you think works best."

"Well, some methods involve counting," replied Doc. "Some have multiple parts, and others use visualization, but it turns out they all accomplish pretty much the same thing. Here, I'll show you a simple version while sitting right in your chairs. Take yourself back to some situation when you were very nervous. A round where you had an unusually good score going would be a perfect example. Have you got the picture? Good.

"Now breathe slowly and fully through your nose and

into your diaphragm. Then breathe out through your mouth, about twice as slowly as you breathed in. As you exhale, do a sequential check of your muscles from head to toe to make sure all of them are fully relaxed. You might notice that one muscle group, such as the hands or forearms, is still tense. This is common in golfers. If so, take another breath and imagine yourself breathing away the tension on the exhale. Give it a try right now if you like and see how it feels."

"Boy, can I ever notice myself relaxing," said Jason after he had tried a few breaths. "I'm going to use that trick the next time I get nervous in a tournament."

"Jason, a smarter approach would be to prepare yourself for stressful situations before they come up," Doc suggested. **"The proper way to learn this technique is in a 'ready position.'**[30] **That means you should do it on the range first, when you're hitting balls, then in a casual round, and finally in game conditions.** Doing it here in the chair will get you started, but **the idea is to work through increasingly higher levels of anxiety until you adapt it to real life."**

"Okay, Doc. I get what you're saying. I'll do that."

"Good. Breathing to relax yourself is an important part of body-talk, fellows, but now, let's hear the expanded version of Kip's tournament story. Would you fill us in, Kip?"

"Well, Doc," Kip began, "it was a roller-coaster ride, to say the least. As for my body language, once I started paying attention, I was amazed at what it told me. If you had time, I'd tell stories until dark, but I'll stick to the important parts.

"I started off by parring the first four holes. The fifth is a dogleg par 5, so I got home in 2 by cutting the corner and made a 20-footer for eagle. In a way that hurt me more than it helped. I guess I got a bit excited and doubled the next hole."

"A bit excited!" Jason exclaimed. "You were out of control. Tell these guys what you did when the putt went in."

Kip laughed as he stood up to demonstrate. In fact, just thinking back to the situation refocused all the energy he had felt at the time. Starting with his fist at hip level, he drove it into the air in a beautiful uppercut that Tiger Woods would have been proud of.

"Not bad," offered Jason. "Now, how about hollering like you did at the qualifier?"

Kip reared back again and struck the air a few more times, ending with a final triumph. "Yeah! Yeah! YEAH!"

Doc turned to Jason and raised his eyebrows. He had a worried look on his face.

Jason shrugged his shoulders. "It's not my fault. I followed your instructions, Doc. After his fist pumps, I talked to him like you told me to. I said, 'I think you've gone over the top, Kip. **How can you use body motions to calm yourself down?'**

"Kip sort of bought into what I was getting at, and he walked a bit slower, but it wasn't enough. I think that's where his double-bogey came from."

"Yeah, it was," Kip confessed. "It wasn't until later that Jason had the time to explain the idea to me a bit better. Anyway, not much happened for the next few holes and then on the 14th green, I forgot to replace my ball mark after one of my playing partners asked me to move it out of his line. I caught my mistake when I was walking to the next tee and almost got sick because I knew it was a two-shot penalty. The wind went right out of my sails."

Once more, Doc looked over at Jason, silently asking what he had said to Kip.

"I followed your instructions again, Doc. This time, his energy level was down, so I said **'How can you use body motions to give yourself more energy?'** Kip clapped his hands a couple of times and said, 'You're right, Jason. I've got to pick it up a bit.' That seemed to help a little and so did walking quicker between shots, although he still ended up shooting 74 in the morning round."

"Jason, I think you directed Kip with excellent questions," Doc pointed out. "Let me tell the others what I said to you at the end of our last session."

Addressing all of the men now, Doc explained; "Tournaments, being a stage of performance, tend to magnify the importance of every shot, so it's easy to experience extremes. However, to play your best at any time, golfers need to have an arousal level that's not too high and not too low.

"Deborah Graham and Jon Stabler have published an interesting book called *The 8 Traits of Champion Golfers*. In it, they explain that the optimum arousal level for golfers is between four and six on a scale of one to 10.[31] By comparison, football players would be at the higher end of the scale, while target shooting requires participants to be at the lower end. In fact there's even an optimum arousal level for everyday activities, like interacting with your family or closing a business deal.

"My instructions were for Jason to act as an observer. If Kip got a bit too excited, Jason's job was to ask him to find a way to calm down a little. Or, if he got too far down, Jason was to ask him how he could pick himself back up. Like I said, Jason did a good job. What I'm wondering now, Kip, is how you made out in the afternoon?"

"Right. So I shot 74 in the morning round," Kip continued. "As you probably know, Doc, in these qualifiers there are about 45 minutes between rounds to grab a bite to eat and relax. I remembered a story about Tiger during the break in his 1996 U.S. Amateur final against Steve Scott. He was five down after 18. He and his coach at the time, Butch Harmon, had a little talk, and Tiger came out in the afternoon with an entirely different attitude, and he won the match.

"Well, for some reason I didn't have Butch's phone number handy – imagine that! So I decided to have a little talk with Jason. He filled me in on your instructions and the reasons behind them, the same way you just explained them to Frank and Andy. He told me you would say that if I waited until after I got outside the four to six arousal level to do something about my body motion, I'd be reacting. It would be better to leave nothing to chance and use proper body motion for the level of arousal I wanted to be in right from the start. I liked that idea. It's sort of like being proactive. It works in sales. So I thought, let's give it a try.

"Then I figured, there have to be more ways to influence my emotions than just clapping and walking, so Jason and I wrote down as many motions as we could think of on the back of a scorecard. I didn't use every one during the afternoon round, but they made me realize what's possible. Here, I kept the scorecard with the list we made on it."

Kip took the scorecard from his pocket and slid it across the table to Doc, who read what they had written down:

- Look down
- Look up
- Shake my head

- Nod my head
- Snap my fingers to a rhythm
- Place my hands confidently on my hips
- Hunch my shoulders
- Walk tall
- Kick the golf bag
- Twirl a club in one hand while walking
- Slam a club into the ground
- Give my caddy a high five
- Walk with a bounce in my step
- Smile
- Frown

Doc looked up after reading the phrases. "That's a pretty good list. What did you do after that?"

"Well, since I'm a big Phil Mickelson fan," said Kip, "I thought about how he always presents himself so well. All throughout his career, he's walked around with a big smile on his face and a bounce in his step, whether he's playing well or poorly. I really admire that, especially considering the tough years he had when the press kept bugging him about being the best player never to win a major.

"By the way," Kip said in an I-told-you-so tone, "it's funny how that smile looks a lot better now that he's got a few majors under his belt. Anyway, Jason and I made a plan. It was to use body motion to create the kind and level of emotion I wanted to have all through the afternoon round, whether things were going my way or not, just like Phil does. The question that Jason came up with for me was this: **What body language do you want to display, regardless of whether you're playing well or poorly?"**

"That's a pretty smart approach. How did it work out?" asked Doc.

"It was great," Kip confirmed. "The very fact that we put together a plan gave me extra confidence. I didn't know for sure how well I'd play – you never do – but I knew I was doing all the little things I needed to give myself a chance. So my mood ended up being nearly perfect, even during the few times in the afternoon that I hit the ball into a bad position or a poor lie."

"I gather you got off to a good start then."

"Good, but not spectacular, Doc. I turned the front side at 1 under with a birdie on nine and started getting a little excited again. Jason reminded me to calm down by being a bit more deliberate. That helped me par number 10 and 11, and I really felt in control. Next thing you know, I rattled off birdies on 12, 13 and 14 like I had done it every day of my life."

"Now at that point you're 2 under for the day, and you've got a qualifying spot wrapped up if you par out, right?" Doc surmised.

"Almost. I was pretty close. So again, using Jason to pace me, three pars later I was standing on the 18th. I knocked my approach shot to about nine feet, leaving me with a very makable birdie. But I got a little uptight since I figured I was near the qualifying score and I never really got a good mind-set for the putt. Of course, you know what happens when you're uncertain. I sort of eased the putt. It never held its line and it rolled about four feet by the hole. So I looked at what I had left and thought, 'How would Phil hit this one?' Then I took some time to make sure I had calmed down, and I knocked it in the center. 74-68, 2 under for the day. It should have been 3 under, but minus 2 got in at that site."

Kip paused, and looked at his friends, "So, I'm going to the U.S. Amateur, Doc, and I've got you and Jason to thank for it!"

"Fantastic, Kip! We're all really proud of you," Doc exclaimed.

Kip, however, still harbored a deep frustration. "But, Doc, like I told you, it was a roller-coaster ride and even though I couldn't be happier about qualifying, I don't like the way I finished. It seems at a certain point when the heat's on I get so stressed that I can't perform like I should. If I had made that last birdie putt there would've been no question about me winning a spot. As it was, I cut it pretty fine. I'm not ready for prime time if I keep that stuff up."

"Whoa. Hold on there, Kip," cautioned Doc. "You're right on the cusp of something very important, so let's be a little patient. You now know that you can use your body as a way of expressing yourself, but did you ever consider that your body wants to speak to you occasionally? The stress you experienced on the second-last putt was just your body's way of trying to tell you something. If you listen carefully to what it was saying you can take your skill to a higher level."

Kip seemed confused, so Doc explained further.

"Let me ask you something," he said. "Was the anxiety you felt over the putt you missed from something you felt in your setup, or was it because you didn't like being in that type of pressure situation?"

"I'm not sure, Doc. Why?"

"Because the cause can help you determine how you should go about finding a solution. If the root of your problem is in your mechanics, your body may have simply noticed that you were aiming right or left, or whatever. The tension would have come from an inner voice screaming that you weren't listening to your own feedback, and you needed to make a physical adjustment. The fix is as simple as going through your routine with your senses open, instead of with inflexible mechanics.

"If, however, you missed the shot due to the anxiety of being in that type of pressure situation, you might benefit from a stress-management technique." Doc put his hand on his chin and thought for a moment. "Stress management," he repeated. "Hmmmm, by the way, Andy, didn't you say last time that your university worker who got stuck way up on a ladder eventually got some help? Just out of curiosity do you mind if I ask what kind of help it was?"

"Oh," Andy said in an unusually quiet voice. "He went to see a professor friend of his named Mike somebody in the psychology department at U of Aurora."

"Really? And what did he do for him?"

"Ahhh, you probably know how those brainy guys work, Doc. Apparently, they had a nice talk first, all about how stress affects our body and our thinking. Then they discussed how to recognize when it's building up. After that the professor told him that together they could overcome his fear of climbing by breaking down the stress into pieces he could cope with. So they got him to climb the first two steps of a ladder, then four steps, then six, and so on just to prove he really could climb a ladder. I guess that's incremental adjustment or something."

"Maybe you're the psychologist, Andy," Doc smiled. "What else?"

"Well, soon they had him climbing ladders with air bags on the ground so he couldn't hurt himself if he fell. Then he climbed a few ladders around his home, where he had done that kind of thing before, and finally he tried climbing again on some work sites. He told me they had him imagining that climbing ladders was really fun. Instead of being afraid, he actually started to enjoy it, and even said there were good views from way up there. From what I heard, in a matter of no time he was running up and down ladders like squirrels run up and down trees."

"So what happened to him?"

"Well, a month later he came back for his job and I gave it to him," said Andy, who then looked off into the distance as if he wanted to end the conversation.

Kip was intrigued. "So, if he was able to come back to work, why do you look so upset?"

"I tell you," said Andy, shaking his head in frustration, "this story is going to be the end of me. It's this way, Kipster," he said, his tone becoming more forceful. "When that kid was originally rescued from the ladder and I saw how messed up he was, I had to let him go. When he came back a few days later for his last paycheck I said to him, 'I'll bet 100 to 1 you'll never get up on a ladder again.' Then, just to make him feel good I threw in a warm fuzzy. 'But you're a good guy, so if you ever get straightened out, I'll give you your summer job back.' Well, wouldn't you know it? He put 20 bucks on the table before he left. He laughed and said, 'If I lose, throw it in with the coffee money, but if I ever learn to climb ladders again I'll be back.' Of course he did and I lost the bet! You know how much that cost me at 100 to 1? How was I supposed to know he was actually going to take me up on the bet or that the mental stuff would really work? I was sure he would never unscramble that noodle of his!"

Kip and the others were beside themselves with laughter. After taking a minute to enjoy Andy's discomfort, Doc's mood changed.

He cocked his head thoughtfully and said, "That professor you called Mike, that wasn't Don Meichenbaum by any chance, was it, Andy?"

"Could have been. Why?"

"Well D.H. Meichenbaum is on staff at the university and he developed Stress Inoculation Training, or SIT.[32] Coach Hollingsworth brings him in to talk to the golf team from time to time. You might have thought you had the odds in your favor on that bet, but with a guy like Meichenbaum working against you, you had no chance," Doc laughed.

"So now you tell me!" Andy groaned. "Where were you last summer when I needed you, Doc?"

"Oh boy, Andy," Kip said with a chuckle. "You never fail to entertain. But I'm glad you told us. I never know which way to turn when I get stressed going down the stretch. I bet I could use that same system to tackle my problem, couldn't I, Doc?"

"You sure could, because Stress Inoculation Training is a classic anxiety reduction technique. Andy's explanation of how it works is pretty accurate, but if you want to read up on it a bit more just do a literature search under Meichenbaum SIT and you'll have all you need."

For the next few minutes the men pestered Andy about other bets he might be willing to take. "100 to 1 the sun comes up tomorrow, Andy. Are you in?" teased Frank. "No? How about 100 to 1 that it gets dark at night? Ha ha ha."

Satisfied that Kip now had a way of dealing with anxiety going down the stretch, Doc focused his attention on the quality effort Jason had turned in assisting Kip during the qualifier. In doing so, he got the men back into the lesson. "I want to compliment you on something, Jason. You did a great job helping Kip in the sectional! What you give out tends to come back, and I believe you'll benefit from your efforts someday."

"Well, I hope that someday is next week," Jason replied.

"You mean in the state junior?"

"Yeah, I've come really close to winning my age group all through junior golf, but never quite pulled it off. The final division is 16 and 17 and I really want to chalk up a win before I move to the next level. It's the best way I can think of to reach my goal of being the top junior in the state."

"Hey, you'll have no problem, Jason," Kip cut in. "In fact, I think you'll be one of the favorites. When you caddied for me I could see you had learned an awful lot from Doc over the past two months. Helping me in my tournament was like applying those lessons in a dry run for your own event next week. I believe all of these experiences are going to catapult you to another level."

"Thanks for the vote of confidence. Sure would be nice if it works out that way," replied Jason.

Everyone was feeling pretty good about how Kip's qualifier had turned out, when Doc noticed Andy was still looking embarrassed from his betting story. In an attempt to redirect his attention, Doc said, "Andy, how about giving us a little summary of what body-talk is all about."

That was all the prodding it took. "No problem, boss. I'll show you how that breathing thing should go first." Standing up, Andy sucked in all the air he could through his nose and filled his chest. When he let his breath out, you could almost hear the thud as his chest fell into his stomach.

"Not bad, Andy," Doc laughed, "although according to the

experts, your diaphragm should puff out, rather than your chest. Breathe into your diaphragm and mentally check for muscle tension as you breathe out. That's proper breathing. How about showing us some body motions?"

Andy stuck his hands in his pockets and lowered his chin until it sat on his chest. His shoulders were hunched as if he was carrying the weight of the world on them while he slowly brushed one foot back and forth aimlessly on the grass. "If I walked around looking like this all day," Andy explained, almost talking into his navel, "my employees would be depressed just looking at me. On the other hand, if I did this…" Andy then did his best imitation of a frenzied dancer, hopping from foot to foot as his arms flailed in all directions. Above hoots of laughter from the others, Andy shouted "…I'D BE OVER THE TOP, and no one would take me seriously."

Then Andy settled down and assumed a calm, purposeful stance. Facing the men squarely and resting his hands on his hips, he concluded: "The proper way to present myself is in a way that gives my customers confidence in my ability. That's what body-talk is about, isn't it, Doc?"

"That's right, Andy, and you belong on Broadway. You've reminded us it's not just the words, but the motions a person uses that influence emotion. And that's a wrap for this evening, fellows."

———————— ◉ ————————

CHAPTER 9

SELF-FULFILLING PROPHECIES

Within a week, Kip's prediction about Jason's game did come true. Advising Kip as a caddy and going through the ups and downs with him at the U.S. Amateur qualifier had consolidated Jason's understanding of Doc's lessons. The process gave Jason the confidence he needed to win the 16- and 17-age division in the 54-hole state junior tournament during the first week of July. He stayed in touch with Doc throughout the event, calling him after each round to discuss his progress. After all, Doc was now one of Jason's traveling companions. However, Doc hadn't seen Jason in person since before the tournament. So not surprisingly, when the men got together at Doc's house for their next session, Doc was eager to see Jason and hear more about his victory.

"Let me congratulate you in person," said Doc as he shook Jason's hand and patted him on the back. "That win is a great feather in your cap, and I'm sure it's just one of many wins in your future. From our conversations during the week, you seemed to be in control of the tournament all the way."

"Yeah. It was kind of weird," Jason replied. "When I got to the tournament site I just knew I was going to play well. I've had high expectations before, but this time I felt like it was a done deal. I think somewhere in the back of my mind I started believing what Kip said to me a couple of weeks ago, and I got really comfortable with myself. His confidence in me made a big difference."

"Hey, you hit the shots buddy, not me. It's your win," Kip said supportively.

"Kip, you need to take some credit, though," commented Doc. "You used a self-fulfilling prophecy last time that was every bit as good as Crenshaw's famous quote in the 1999 Ryder Cup."

"Crenshaw?" Kip asked.

"Yes, Crenshaw. Let me remind you of the story. In the 1999 Ryder Cup, the U.S. team was down by a score of 10 points to 6 going into the last day of play. Ben Crenshaw, the team captain, said in an interview after the matches, 'Call it what you like. I just had this feeling we were going to win this thing and last night I told my players so.' And they did win! The U.S. players won 8½ out of 12 possible points, producing the greatest comeback in Ryder Cup history. Considering Jason's results, your prediction last week was every bit as good."

Kip nodded playfully. "Sure, the sound of me and Crenshaw being mentioned in the same sentence has a nice ring to it. The only difference is, if I had his money I could afford to burn mine. Really, though, don't you think the results of the Ryder Cup and Jason's tournament had more to do with ability than anything anyone said?"

"You think so?" Doc questioned. "Let's say Crenshaw had said what many journalists were writing at the time: 'Well guys, it looks like our goose is cooked. There's no way we can win tomorrow because we're just too far behind.' How do you think the U.S. team would've performed the next day? Or, what if before Jason's tournament, he had said, 'I'll play, but I really haven't got a chance to beat all those other good players.' Obviously he wouldn't have played with very much confidence, but self-fulfilling prophecies are more than just wishful thinking. There's actually evidence to explain their effectiveness.

"Frank, do you want to tell our friends here about the research I asked you to do, and the origin of self-fulfilling prophecies?"

"Sure, Doc," Frank replied. As might be expected of a former teacher, Frank took some notes out of his pocket for reference and began. "The concept of a self-fulfilling prophecy is rooted in a character named Pygmalion, created by the ancient Roman poet Ovid. Pygmalion was a sculptor who carved the form of a beautiful woman out of ivory. It was so lifelike, he fell in love with the statue and offered it gifts. Eventually, he prayed to Venus, the goddess of beauty and love, who took pity on Pygmalion and brought the statue to life so they could be together."

"Why was that Pygmalion guy playing with statues?" Andy asked. "Couldn't he get a date with a real girl?"

"Settle down, Andy, or you'll have to stay after class," said Frank, feigning sternness. "Throughout the centuries, the idea of bringing wishes to life has been written about so often that the Pygmalion effect has become folklore. That's why some people think the idea is no more than pie-in-the-sky thinking. However, in modern times, researchers Robert Rosenthal and Lenore Jacobson proved that reality can be influenced by expectations.[33] In one set of classic experiments, they told teachers that certain students were gifted, even though the students' abilities were the same as a control group. The students who were expected to perform better did, because, it was discovered, the teachers treated those students differently, and the students, in turn, began seeing themselves differently. As a result of this study, and others, what literature used to describe as a Pygmalion effect has now come to be called a self-fulfilling prophecy.

"The lesson to be learned is that regardless of talent, anyone can improve their performance simply by creating healthy expectations."

"Excuse me, fellows," said Doc, "this would be a good time to explain the pattern behind a self-fulfilling prophecy. So let me steal a moment before Frank continues. **First, a person says something about the future that sets up an expectation for themselves or other people. Then, they consciously or subconsciously give cues that are consistent with that expectation. Finally, they, or others, start matching their cues to the desired outcome, and the prophecy comes to pass.**

"For instance, when Ben Crenshaw communicated his expectations in the '99 Ryder Cup, his team started to get in sync with the suggestion. Before they knew it, they were all doing things that reinforced the idea in each other that they were going to win. That's why quite often the suggestion becomes reality," Doc concluded. "Okay, Frank, go on."

"One amazing thing I learned from looking into this subject," Frank explained, "is that **self-fulfilling prophecies can be either positive or negative.** That's scary! So I wrote down this question for myself: What negative self-fulfilling prophecies have I developed in the past that might still be working against me? Thinking about it for a while, I noticed the jokes I make, such as, 'I'll never get rich doing this,' or 'The autograph hunters will never be after me,' redirect my thinking away from the results I'd actually like to achieve. I used to say those things because I thought they'd get a laugh. But now I don't think what they do to me is so funny.

"Besides what I say out loud, I noticed I have a few persistent subconscious thoughts. For example: 'I'll never learn to hit a flop shot like the pros do,' or 'If I had to deal with the pressure they face, I'd probably fold like an accordion.' So after doing the research you suggested, I decided that from now on, all my self-fulfilling prophecies are going to be positive ones. But that's as far as I got, Doc. I know we should use self-fulfilling prophecies, but I don't quite know how to put them together."

"Hey Frank," said Doc, "you did a very nice job with the research. Thanks. It was interesting and well presented. I'm also impressed you realized self-fulfilling prophecies include your subconscious thoughts, as well as what you say out loud. As for how to construct them, there is a right way, just like there's a right way to set goals. I'll show you how so you can have some fun with the technique anytime you want.

"When you're creating a self-fulfilling prophecy, take a light-hearted approach and imagine you're using a recipe for a triple-layer cake.

"The base layer is a conjecture, like one of the following:
I bet you...
It's a possibility that...
I have this feeling...

"The middle layer is the action that you would like to see come to pass:
I could make four birdies in a row if I really tried...
I'm going to get a big break...
I'll become very influential someday...

"The layer that tops it all off is a reason, or plan, that strengthens the belief:

...because my putter gets hot every once in a while.

...because I'm going to turn over every stone until something works.

...by building a network of experts to work with.

"Quite often, people get good results without completing the third step. However, that step is especially worthwhile because it gives your brain a reason for believing something that it didn't, up until that point. The reason doesn't have to be perfect, either. It can even be whimsical, which is typical of self-fulfilling prophecies. You could simply say, 'because I deserve it.'

"Of course, you know what's coming next, don't you gentlemen? Since you've learned how self-fulfilling prophecies are created, it would be good for you to write one or two in your books now, so that you develop a command of the skill."

Frank still wondered what approach he should use. "What do you think's best, Doc? Should we write about our golf games or about everyday issues?"

"It really doesn't matter, Frank," replied Doc. "It's the exercise that's important, and the skill you develop is transferable from one part of your life to another. From what I understand, though, your handicap has come down two shots since our first meeting. Your friends here have also told me that you're much more excited about your game than you've been for a few years. You could simply make a prophecy about where it's going from here."

Using that kind of encouragement, Doc asked Kip, Jason, Andy and Frank to create their own self-fulfilling prophecies over the next few minutes.

Frank wrote: "*I just might...lower my handicap even more....*

After all, now that Doc's helping me clear away the cobwebs, there's no telling what I might be able to accomplish."

Andy came up with: "*You never know... if I could just catch that hard spot on the 11th fairway... I might be able to scoot a drive right up on the green one of these days."*

Jason's self-fulfilling prophecy was free-spirited: "*There's a good possibility...I'll play on the tour someday...after all, somebody's got to be a star."*

When they were finished, Jason asked a question the other men were thinking. "Doc, we all know self-fulfilling prophecies come true from time to time, but if they were such sure bets, all we'd have to do to become the next Tiger Woods is sit around and make great big predictions. Obviously that doesn't work, so what do we do to make sure we don't end up disappointed most of the time?"

"You maintain a touch of realism, Jason," advised Doc. "Self-fulfilling prophecies may not need to be as serious as proper goals are, but they must still contain a little bit of realism in order to take hold. It's also helpful to understand that the objectives of a self-fulfilling prophecy are first, to keep you in motion, and second, to help you grow. If you combine these ideas, you'll get great results.

"For example, Tiger's father, who was a master at using self-fulfilling prophecies, didn't predict major championships when his son was in the cradle. His first goal was to raise a good person who could face life's challenges confidently.[34] So the things Earl Woods said to his son as a child led Tiger in that direction. Next, when Tiger showed promise in golf, his father pointed him to the next rung on the ladder. He would say things like, 'I like the way you are swinging the club. It won't be long before you are hitting the ball a ton.'[35] When Tiger started showing unusual athletic ability, his father took him a step further by suggesting that he'd be able to call on a special gear, because he had that unique ability."[36]

"Man, have we seen that extra gear over the years!" Frank exclaimed.

"We sure have," agreed Doc. "Once it became obvious that Tiger was going to be very, very famous, Earl Woods made what was probably his greatest prediction of all. He said, 'Tiger will take the game of golf to all nations of the world.' It was a great statement because it allowed Tiger's wide range of developing abilities to find an outlet, which Tiger needed if he was going to keep growing. Of course, that's exactly what's happened. We see this not only in his worldwide playing schedule, but also through his international branding efforts and endeavors like the Tiger Woods Learning Center.

"In short, taking golf to all nations of the world was really only a small step for Tiger once his career had hit full stride, although it would have been too large a leap earlier in his career. You can see that each of the predictions, from first to last, kept Tiger constantly moving forward.

"So another lesson each of us can learn from this is quite simple. **Regardless of our abilities, a self-fulfilling prophecy that's slightly challenging will provide us with a picture of success to grow into.**"

Kip stood up and began to pace. "So if I understand this correctly, Doc, a self-fulfilling prophecy is a way of talking about the future that directs our thoughts toward an outcome we want to achieve, something like goals do. Yet they aren't as tightly bound by the rules of being specific, measurable, realistic and having a time frame."

"Yes, that would be a good way to explain it. You know, Kip, you've heard of some people being described as creative right-brain people, while the more logical, step-by-step types are referred to as left-brain people, right?"

"Yeah, I've heard that idea. What about it?"

"Well, you could think of setting goals, with all its rules and steps, as being a left-brain process. You could also see making self-fulfilling prophecies, which are more whimsical and free-flowing, as being a right-brain process. Most of us tend to accentuate one side or the other, but developing them both is like finding the mate to a two-piece puzzle. One needs the other to be complete."

"Hey, now I know where Tiger gets one of his extra gears from," Frank said with dawning realization. "He's been using both halves of the puzzle, as Doc puts it. The first piece of the puzzle is his goals. He's got Nicklaus's records to motivate him, plus other goals that he says are even higher than the public could imagine. The other piece of the puzzle is the self-fulfilling prophecy. Tiger's had a steady diet of them since he was a kid. I'm sure that in itself it isn't the total reason for his success, but it's just another one of those little things that Tiger builds into his repertoire. And everyone thinks they can get to the top just by grooving their swing. Fat chance!"

"You know what? Frank's right," said Kip. "The goal-setting I've done in training courses always seemed as if it was just a bit forced. On the other hand, the daydream goals I've had since childhood feel more natural. They're a product of my child-like right-brain side, aren't they? Sure. I can't count the times I said as a kid, 'When I grow up I'm going to do this, or be that,' and a lot of those things have come true. So if we add self-fulfilling prophecies to the goals we set earlier, I bet they would work a lot better, wouldn't they, Doc?"

"They sure would," Doc confirmed. "In fact, the logical goals you set a few weeks ago have been waiting restlessly ever since for their emotional counterparts to arrive. Instead of keeping them waiting, you might want to reinforce them now with your new understanding of how the two complement each other. **"What self-fulfilling prophecies can you create to complement the goals you've set?"**

"Let me think this through a bit more," said Kip, who was still pacing. "If my ambition is to qualify for the Masters by finishing first or second in the U.S. Amateur, and I want to add a self-fulfilling prophecy, I could say, *One of these days...I'm going to jump up and win something big...because I'll just ride a streak when it comes along.* Hmmmph. It's amazing how just saying that makes me feel a lot more confident and relaxed about my goal."

Kip had taken his chair now, but was rocking lazily on its two rear legs and thinking back. "Remember the day we first met, Doc? You told Jason that working on the fundamentals wasn't regressing. It was *progressing* to a child-like state. Now that we've learned how to think and how to talk, is that where all this is heading?"

"You might say so, Kip. The last fundamental of success is How To Play, which is all about being like a child again. Children are the masters of learning, and they do much of it while playing. I know you're going to have fun with those lessons because your ability to look at life the way a child does hasn't gone away. It's just been collecting dust for a few years."

"Well, you know, Doc, when I was growing up, my dad used to say: You'll never be happier than when your feet are beneath your father's table. He meant that the years of our youth are the best years of our lives. Later on, I came to realize it also meant that the advice I heard from my father was some of the best I would ever hear." Kip eased his chair forward until all four legs were on the ground and his feet were firmly planted beneath the patio table. "So, Doc, I can hardly wait."

The 3rd Fundamental of Success

HOW TO PLAY

CHAPTER 10

ABSORBING

"Jump in, guys. It's time we headed off to Doc's again," said Kip as the men gathered around his car in the parking lot. "By the way, how about Tiger's win today? He really put on a show, didn't he?"

"No wonder he won," Andy huffed as he paused by an open car door. "Did you see who was trying to catch him? I can't stand that goofball. Just the way he walks bugs me, and did you hear his interview after? What a wimp!"

"Well, why don't you tell us how you really feel?" Frank teased, resting his hand on the door latch. "I thought your so-called goofball gave Tiger a pretty good run. He hit a couple of super iron shots when it counted, and there are a lot of people who would say Tiger won the tournament more than anyone lost it. For my money, he showed a lot of poise."

"Are we talking about the same guy?" Andy snorted. "As far as I'm concerned he's a complete idiot."

"Well, maybe beauty's in the eye of the beholder," Frank countered. "His swing has such great rhythm! As a matter of fact, I've been trying to visualize taking the club back nice and slow, then accelerating through the same way."

"Have fun, pal. There's no way I'd want to imitate anything he does," Andy replied, getting into the car and closing the door.

"Really? Even if it meant you could improve?" Frank said from the front seat. I bet if Doc were here, he'd say, **'If you liked this person, instead of disliked him, what would you have learned already?'"**

"Boys, boys," chided Kip.

"Onward, James," Jason called out from the back seat.

• • •

When their vehicle eased into Doc's driveway, Doc met the men as he often did. This time, however, Doc had a request. "Would the rest of you please wait here while I walk Kip to the backyard alone? I'll come back to get each of you after that."

"That's okay with us, Doc," the men replied, puzzled but unconcerned.

While Jason listened to Andy and Frank wind down their conversation on the merits of the player who lost to Tiger that afternoon, Doc walked with Kip along the side of the house, past the tool shed and toward the patio table. They exchanged pleasantries as they went, but each time Kip said something, Doc responded in a slightly quieter tone. Kip, in turn, reduced the level of his voice to match Doc's, so that by the time he was seated at the patio table, Kip noticed he was speaking very quietly, breathing calmly and was extremely relaxed. He sat down in his chair, not even bothering to ask Doc the reason for this change in pattern, and Doc walked back to the remaining men. This time, Doc motioned for Andy to follow him, and repeated the process.

When Doc showed up with Jason, Andy and Kip were sitting quietly, taking in the surroundings and noticing certain things they had never really paid attention to before. Frank was the last person to join the quiet group and sit down.

"Thanks for being so patient," Doc said to the men. "Isn't it a beautiful evening?"

It certainly was a beautiful evening, and there were numerous things for the men to take in. They saw treetops silhouetted against sculpted white clouds and blue sky. They heard the gentle swishing sound leaves make while swaying in the breeze.

At each seat were the usual refreshments Doc put out for them every week. An additional item this time was a sprig of mint, positioned neatly beside each glass. One of the men picked up the bumpy textured leaf out of curiosity, and squeezed it until its moisture created a green stain on his fingertips. Noticing this, the others imitated his action. The resulting scent that reached their noses was pleasant and sweetly refreshing.

Doc had orchestrated this sequence for a reason. He wanted the men to **quietly absorb experiences through all five senses – the basic human tools for learning about everything around us.** As they sipped their drinks, the men experienced the last of the five senses – taste. **Sight, sound, smell, touch and taste**. They had absorbed an experience for each.

"Doc, are you trying to run a Montessori school here?" Frank quizzed. "The way you always lay out the table, chairs and place settings reminds me of how those classrooms are set up. Everything is clean and orderly to help students absorb experiences better."

"I'm glad you noticed. In case some of you aren't familiar with the concepts of Maria Montessori, who was one of the world's most innovative child educators, I'll explain her stages of learning. Understanding them will make anything you attempt easier to learn.

Montessori showed that learning is a three-phase process. The phases are absorbing, connecting and applying.

"The reason I sat you down so deliberately and quietly today was so that you'd be in a receptive mood. Being receptive is essential to the first learning phase.

"In the same way you took in everything around you just now, a very young child sitting in the middle of a busy room is indiscriminately receptive to everything around him. He absorbs through every one of his senses.[37] Children don't develop the habit of filtering out certain experiences and retaining others the way adults do until later in life.[38] If they did, they would be hindering their development.

"In golf, as in the learning of any skill," continued Doc, "absorbing the nuances of all the factors outside and inside of you is the first phase of learning.

"Tiger's father taught him at an early age to develop the habit of considering every possible external condition pertinent to a shot. Together they analyzed hazards, wind, lies, and even soil conditions.[39]

"Internal considerations are also important – both the physical and the mental ones. Physically, how do your muscles feel? How does your posture and setup change from day to day? Mentally, what's your mood, discipline, fatigue level, patience, preparedness, anxiety, creativity and ambition?

"Most people think they take into account every condition for whatever they do, whether it's playing golf or working at their job. However, only when you can describe all of your conditions in as much detail as someone like a climatologist is able to describe the weather, for instance, can you be certain you've absorbed all that's available."

"A climatologist?" asked Jason.

"Sure. A climatologist is a weatherman with a larger vocabulary. He observes weather more precisely, and uses more words for snow, for example, than the average person does."

"Such as?" Jason prodded.

"Such as flurries, powder, corn, ice, firn, snizzle, hail, slush, penitentes, and – are you ready for this? – watermelon snow."

Jason covered his ears in mock protest. "Stop! I'm sorry I asked."

Undeterred, Doc went on. "Climatologists have developed these words so they can communicate the details of climate more accurately to everyone, from farmers to pilots to resort owners. People in those professions depend on specific information like that for their livelihood, while most of us would simply think of snow as being white and cold.

"High achievers also view their internal and external variables in higher detail than the average person does.[40] A case in point is Jack Nicklaus. He was keenly aware that pressure situations could cause him to rush a shot. So when he noticed those situations developing he would slow his pace down. Of course, most of us would say it's easy for us to tell when we're rushing a shot. But, by and large, the average person doesn't absorb as many subtle cues, or pick them up as early, as a professional does. In fact, they don't even realize how many things there are to absorb. That's why you should ask yourself: **What internal and external conditions do higher achievers in my field consider that I should too?**"

"I know for sure that when I'm really playing well, my senses are much sharper," said Jason. "I notice all kinds of little things."

"Exactly. And if you keep an open mind to what your senses

want to tell you, you'll start seeing more and more variables, just like Tiger and Nicklaus do," said Doc.

"That would be neat," said Jason. "I'm game for anything that would help me be sharp more often. What should we do after that?"

"Move to phase two," Doc answered. **If phase one is a time of gathering, phase two is a time of discovery.** According to Montessori, in this phase of learning, we repeatedly act out connections between our absorbed information. Children do this through physical activities as simple as trying to touch their toes, or as complex as using a chair to climb up on a counter in search of cookies. By testing the various ways that information can be connected, threads of understanding begin linking everything we've absorbed."[41]

"You know, Doc, that's interesting," Kip remarked. "I heard that Annika Sorenstam once asked Tiger Woods to show her his arsenal of golf shots. Afterward, she said that Tiger considered more options and was able to play more shots than anyone she had ever met. Is Tiger's approach what you mean by connecting?"

"It is," Doc confirmed. "Many people say Tiger's success is based on his athletic gifts and they think they could never imitate him, but they forget about his attention to the basics. At one point, Tiger used to ask his golf pro to teach him a new shot almost every day. Then he'd go out and experiment until he could hit the shot.

"Tiger earned his 'gifts' by absorbing everything he could, and then linking the information in as many different ways as possible.[42] The result is the variety of shots he uses today, and that formula is a foundation for anyone's development."

"I see. So our ability to learn goes back to connecting," Kip concluded, "and that process goes all the way back to absorbing information, doesn't it?"

"Yes," confirmed Doc, "and to go back even further, **your ability to absorb depends on being receptive to any and all stimuli around you. This not only includes the things you absorb through your five senses, but what you can absorb from people as well.**"[43]

Andy felt a sharp kick to his leg under the table, and looked up. "Whaaat?" he said, searching out the offender.

"See. I told you so," said Frank. "That pro you called a goof-ball today has one of the best swings on tour. What Doc's saying is that you could watch him forever and never pick anything up because you're not receptive to him." Then Frank added a conciliatory thought. "But I guess you're not the only one who shuts out other people. I do the same thing myself sometimes, so I'm going to make a point of getting away from that habit. It can't be doing me any good."

"I must be missing part of an earlier conversation, fellows," said Doc, "although I'm figuring out that you realize you're missing a lot of opportunities. Even a ballerina, who looks so dainty you'd normally never identify with her, has something to offer. Her grace and muscle control is something you could emulate, but only if you appreciate her talent without prejudice. Her precision would certainly complement the power you want to generate in your golf swing. So I encourage you to be open to positive influences from the most unlikely people. You'll find yourself refreshed by their talents."

Andy assured Doc his suggestion would land on fertile soil. "I don't want Frank kicking me anymore," he said.

"Good. Then you're ready for **the third learning phase. It consists of applying the connections you've made to real-life situations**. That would mean actually hitting a new shot you've been practicing in a situation that means something. If it's not a tournament, it could be a game with a friendly wager on it, but it has to be a situation that bears a consequence. If you're playing the type of golf where you give yourself three- and four-footers, or nothing worse than a double, you're short-changing your opportunity to learn."

"You know what?" interjected Kip. "I seem to remember something like that in Harvey Penick's *Little Red Book*." Kip paused for a moment. "Oh, yeah, now I know what it was. He said a young married couple came to him one day bragging that their son had made his first birdie. When Penick asked how long the putt was, they said it was only two feet so they gave their son a gimme to make sure he didn't experience failure. Penick looked at them and said, 'I've got bad news for you. Junior still hasn't made his first birdie.'"[44]

"Good story," said Doc, "but a sad one, because that young-ster was denied the opportunity to fail, or the opportunity to apply, as we've been phrasing it. I'm sure that like all parents his mom and dad meant well, but in trying to protect their child from disappointment, they took away a valuable chance to learn.[45] The point is, the threads of learning aren't finally fused together until we complete the third phase.

"That idea also helps answer the question about why some people who practice a lot don't improve their performance. The average player beating balls on the range hits the same shot over and over, narrowing and eliminating variations of movement. He looks for results as if he were in the third phase of learning. What he forgets is that the practice range is primarily for the second phase of learning. It's the experimentation ground. Shots aren't mastered on the range. They're discovered. Only those who go on to apply their experiments in game conditions master the skills and make real progress – which brings me around to Jack Nicklaus." Looking at Frank, Doc said, "Do you remember the stories about how Nicklaus used to get ready for tournaments?"

"Oh, I sure do, Doc," answered Frank. "Back then, Nicklaus made it his business to go to tournament sites in advance and prepare for events by working on specific shots. All the keen professionals do it now, but in his day no one prepared like Nicklaus did."

"That's right," said Doc. "And going back to Montessori, she would have said that he was absorbing the unique conditions, connecting the information to decide which shots were necessary, and then applying them during the tournament. When you think about it, it's easy to understand how anyone who prepared so thoroughly, not just Nicklaus and Woods, would be confident[46] in their ability to perform when the pressure is on.

"Now," said Doc, "It's time to get you into action. Knowing all this, you can probably understand that some of your past failures might be a result of failing to go through all three learning stages. So, thinking about one of those past situations, ask yourself this question: **Which one of the three learning stages – absorbing, connecting and applying – would have helped me succeed in that situation if I would have put more time or effort into the appropriate stage?**

"Kip? Jason? Frank? Andy? Can you see how answering that question would help?"

"Yeah, Doc, there sure are a few things that might have turned out differently if I had known this before," Andy replied. Then he paused to get Doc's attention. "But you know, Doc, it's not like I'm hurt or anything, it's just, well, until just now you haven't used any of our names even once today." Andy slowly wiped an imaginary tear from the corner of his eye and sniffed. "That's not like you. Are you trying to tell us something?"

"Mmmm," Doc replied, scratching the top of his head. "Now that you mention it, I've noticed that myself. What's your name again?"

The group laughed. "Seriously, though," Doc continued, "there are two reasons. First, I wanted you to see that the answers to the questions we've discussed apply to everyone, not just to one or the other of you. If I had used your names while answering questions, the others might not have listened as closely. This way…"

"I get it," Andy jumped in. "This way we absorb more," he said, completing Doc's thought for him.

"Right, and second, without hearing anyone's name, I knew you'd use your imaginations a little more than usual. That's good preparation, because Imagining is the topic of our next lesson."

• • •

"All aboard who's coming aboard," called Kip a short while later. "See you in a couple of weeks, Doc. Bye for now."

"Okay, guys. Next time," Doc said, waving goodbye.

Before their vehicle had traveled even a block, Jason blurted out, "Watermelon snow? Was Doc just pulling our legs today, or is that really a special type of snow?"

"Beats me," answered Kip, "but here, take my cell phone and connect to the Internet. Look up snow on one of those online dictionaries."

Jason, using Kip's phone, tapped away. "Okay, here we go…

Snow...let's see...types of snow.... Well, just listen to this. Watermelon snow: A reddish-pink colored snow that smells like watermelons, and is caused by a red-colored, green alga called chlamydomonas nivalis.[47] That's a mouthful. Why in the world would anyone bother to think about smelling snow?"

"Don't know, but obviously it allowed someone to learn more about that frozen white stuff than they knew before," Kip surmised. "On the other hand, it's interesting that a person could learn about snow using the sense of smell. In a sales course I once took we were told about a very successful consultant who developed a business called Five Sensing. He would show manufacturers how to improve their product presentations by appealing to sight, sound, smell, taste and touch.

"One company he helped used to put sheets of sandpaper in cardboard packages for retail markets. He told them to cut a little window in the packaging so customers could touch the grit before making their purchase. The brand outsold all others until the competition caught on.

"One of the reasons this consultant was successful was that he was thorough. Instead of stopping after he had one success, he walked through every product the company had, looking to see how many of the five senses could be applied. Not every sense applied to every product, but enough did to make the company very profitable, and the consultant very rich."

"So what are we supposed to do? Start sniffing our golf clubs?" Andy asked sarcastically.

"Maybe," Frank shot back. "When we smell smoke coming out of your ears, we'll know your game stinks and we won't take you as a partner."

"Very funny!"

"Hey, I know," said Jason. "I could try paying attention to the vibration of the club when I make contact with the ball. That's the sense of touch. I usually just judge my shots by how they fly and where they end up, but looking for other things would give me more feedback, wouldn't it?"

Frank agreed. "I bet it would, and just like Doc said, higher achievers pay attention to stuff like that when other people don't. You know, apparently the first time Jack Nicklaus saw Arnold Palmer, Arnie was hitting balls in the rain. When Nicklaus wrote about it later, he said even though it was raining, he watched Palmer hit shots for about an hour because he was so amazed at the sound coming off his club face."[48]

Frank gave Andy another sharp kick to his leg.

"Whaaaaaaat?"

"Don't you see? Even though Arnie was Jack's rival, and didn't have the most classic swing in the world, Nicklaus wasn't so big-headed that he said 'There's no way I'm imitating that swing or anything he does.' Jack absorbed Palmer's excellence when others didn't – even out in the rain, and that's another reason why Jack Nicklaus became Jack Nicklaus! Get it?"

"Oh…. Oh yeah!"

CHAPTER 11

IMAGINING

As the men walked to Doc's backyard on Sunday evening, Frank chatted eagerly about that week's topic. "I'm glad we're finally getting a chance to talk about visualizing, Doc. I want to see shots exactly the way those tour pros do."

"Hey, Doc, it doesn't sound like you and Frank are on the same page," Kip interjected. "He just said this lesson is about visualizing, but your book says it's about imagining. What's the difference between the two?"

"Those terms do get a bit confusing, don't they?" replied Doc. "I guess it would be useful to sort them out. Visualizing is really a simpler form of imagining. Or, if you prefer, imagining is a richer form of visualizing.

"If you visualize yourself standing on a mountaintop, you only see yourself in that place. On the other hand, if you imagine yourself on a mountaintop you actually feel as though you're there. You sense the sun and wind on your face, plus the exhilaration of being on top of the world.

"Regardless of the terminology, though, **this lesson is about the art of creating pictures. The more vivid the pictures**

are of what you want to achieve, the easier it is for you to work toward them, so we'll deal with visualizing first, then with imagining."

As Doc finished speaking, the men were seating themselves at the patio table. But Andy, ever the prankster, wasn't quite ready to settle in for the day's lesson. He pulled away Jason's chair just as his young friend tried to sit down. An instant later Andy was laughing uncontrollably at Jason's lanky body lying in a heap on the ground.

"Only you would do something like that, Andy," Jason chided. "Just for that, next time we play you're not getting any shots."

"I'm glad you didn't hurt yourself," Doc said kindly, reaching down to grab Jason's arm. Andy, despite his prank, took the other arm and helped Jason to his feet. "However, I'd like to say that what just happened here is an excellent demonstration of visualizing."

"How's that?" Jason asked, dusting himself off.

"Well, when you tried to sit down you couldn't see the chair because, naturally, your back was to it. Therefore, you must have moved your body toward the picture of the chair you had in your mind, instead of the actual chair. That shows just how important mental pictures are in providing instructions for our bodies to act.

"High achievers are excellent at using pictures to direct their performance. So it should be no surprise that by looking at how Tiger and Nicklaus use pictures, we can help ourselves perform better."

"I think I know what you mean," said Jason. "Every once in a while I get over a putt and I just know I'm going to make it. I can almost see it going in before it happens. I'd love for you to show me a way to make that happen more often."

"Super, because there's a great quote by Nicklaus I'd like you to hear. It describes the pictures he conjures up before each shot." Doc opened his copy of Jack Nicklaus's *Golf My Way* to a page he had marked and began reading:

'I never hit a shot, even in practice, without having a very sharp, in-focus picture of it in my head. It's like a color movie. First I "see" the ball where I want it to finish, nice and white and sitting up on the bright green grass. Then the scene quickly changes and I "see" the ball going there: its path, trajectory, and shape, even its behavior on landing. Then there's a sort of fade-out, and the next scene shows me making the kind of swing that will turn the previous images into reality.'[49]

"That's neat," said Kip. "It sounds like Nicklaus used three different pictures, or 'scenes,' as he called them."

"Right," agreed Doc, "and if you think about it, **every achievement is made up of three similar pictures. You could call one the Goal Picture – where Nicklaus wanted the ball to end up. The second one is the Plan Picture – what the ball had to do to get to the target. The third is the Success Picture – Nicklaus seeing himself performing the task successfully.**

"If you were a businessperson, for example, trying to bring a new product to market, there would be three comparable pictures. The first might be your vision of the product in every home across the country. The second would be the plan to produce, market and distribute the product. The third would be the image of yourself as the leader who makes all the decisions to bring this about. Since you're trying to accomplish something yourself, it would be interesting to consider this question: **Do you currently have clear pictures for each stage of your goal?**

"Once you do that and look at Jack's pictures again, it's easy to see that all three of them are connected. That means **when you change one picture, the other two must be adjusted, or the change you're looking for won't take effect.**"

"Andy, did you hear that?" Kip asked, turning to his friend. "When you change one picture you have to adjust the other two! We've often told you your love affair with that 14 handicap is what's holding you back. Since we started this program, your goal has been to hit the ball straighter and you've been making some progress. You've even had some really good stretches, but it never seems to show up in your final score. I wonder if that's because you don't really want your handicap to come down, just in case you aren't competitive in our money games. Maybe you need to adjust the picture of your handicap if you want the picture of your ball flight to change."

Although Andy knew these comments were probably right on the mark, he responded with a challenge. "Not so fast there, buddy. You're no different. You say you want to win the U.S. Amateur, and we all know how good you are and everything, but I think you've been neglecting those finesse shots you have to learn. Maybe you need to adjust the picture of how you're going to achieve your goal?"

"I've actually been working harder than you might think," Kip asserted. "But I'll buy your argument – to a point. I do need to experiment a little more with a couple of shots." Then Kip paused.

"Tell you what, though. I'll keep picturing my plan if you start picturing the scores that'll lower your handicap. Deal?" asked Kip, reaching across to shake Andy's hand.

"Yeaaah, it's a deal," Andy replied grudgingly, knowing he'd been had. After all, the safety net his high handicap offered was now in jeopardy. Andy's only hope of saving face now was to up the ante for Kip. "But I'll tell you what. If you do what you say you're going to, I expect to see you in front of the cameras when they televise the Amateur in a couple of weeks. Got it?"

"Got it, buddy," Kip winked. "Better get on with the lesson, Doc. Before the cameras roll, I need to know if Tiger uses pictures the same way Jack does."

"Ummhmm, sort of," Doc resumed. "But no two people do things in exactly the same way. So, while Tiger, like all great athletes, uses pictures, it's his picture of the target while putting that you'll probably find the most interesting. He learned the technique from his father, and here's how they used it.

"First Tiger would look at the hole, then the ball. When Tiger looked down at the ball, his father would ask, 'Do you see the picture of the hole?' If the answer was no, the process was repeated. If the answer was yes, Tiger's father would have him simply stroke the ball to the picture.[50] The important point is that Tiger could see the target in his mind's eye before he took action. It's a wonderful technique to use, whether you're hitting a putt or attempting anything else."

"Interesting," said Frank. "There's just one problem. Nicklaus and Tiger obviously have an amazing ability to create pictures. I don't seem to be able to do that."

"Frank, **you can create pictures much more easily than**

you think. It's simply a matter of using words in the color-ful, descriptive way children use them. It's a technique we'll refer to as Comparing, which uses the magical words 'like' and 'as.'

"Psychologists have learned that we change our language as our mental abilities develop.[51] Unfortunately for adults, our choice of words serves up fewer vivid pictures as our thought processes become more sophisticated. Children, on the other hand, inevitably use comparisons to explain their world, and it's this use of comparisons that has the potential to create fabulous pictures for us.

"For instance, every child wants to grow up, but instead of saying 'I'm going to grow up to be 6 feet 2 inches tall,' they tend to say things like 'I'm going to grow up to be big, just like my dad,' or 'as big as a house.' A person can certainly visualize the term 'as big as a house' much more easily than the adult abstract concept of measurement – in this case, 6 feet 2 inches. By using those magical words ourselves, it's easy to imitate the way children speak and come up with great images.

"Here, I'll take you through a couple of exercises and you'll see what I mean. Let's say the sentence is: The ball landed on the green. By itself, this sentence doesn't generate much of a picture, but let's try making the landing of the ball more descriptive. The ball landed on the green like…"

Doc looked at each of the men. "Come on, guys, I know you can finish off the sentence. Just say anything that comes to your mind after the word 'like.'"

"… like a feather?" offered Frank.

"Not bad. What else?"

"... like a balloon," suggested Andy.

"Ummhmm," Doc nodded. "Can you describe the balloon?"

"... like a water balloon – as in SPLAT! That sucker ain't going nowhere when it lands."

"Oh boy, Andy," Doc chuckled, "you're a treat. But see, that wasn't so hard, was it? In fact, choosing perfect words isn't necessary with this technique. Almost any descriptive word or phrase will create a picture, and you'll naturally refine the words until you find an image you like. The benefit of this technique is that your embellished descriptions will help you hold pictures in your mind, just like Tiger's father helped him hold a picture of the target he was putting to.

"Now," said Doc, "let's try another example, using the word 'as.' We'll start with this sentence: I'm going to keep my head still. Let's turn that into I'm going to keep my head as still as..."

"... as a block of cement!" Andy followed up.

Frank jumped up from his seat in protest as fast as a coiled spring. "Doc, it's not fair to let Andy answer that question. He's a blockhead already." Jason and Kip were in stitches. They both reached across the patio table to high-five Frank, showing their approval for his zinger.

"No comment," said Doc, who also enjoyed Frank's theatrics. "In any case, isn't that an easier way of telling your body what to do than saying I'm going to keep my head perfectly still?"

"It sure is, Doc," Andy grinned. "It's really easy to see how using comparisons improves our ability to visualize. But we better move on to imagining. These guys are getting jealous of my razor-sharp mind."

"Okay. Let's do that. This next technique is called **Layering,** which is exactly what it sounds like – the process of applying more layers. Of course, you're going to ask what kinds of layers a person can apply. The answer is **first, you can find more layers of vision. Second, you can apply layers of the remaining senses – sound, touch, taste and smell. Finally, you can apply mood layers.**[52] When you do all this, you progress from visualizing to imagining. Let's look at Nicklaus's three scenes again to understand the concept: 'First, I 'see' where I want it to finish, nice and white and sitting up on the bright green grass.'

"Normally, if you ask people where they want the ball to end up, they'd point to a spot and simply say, 'Over there.' What's more, there's a good chance their picture would be in black and white. On the other hand, Nicklaus paints three layers in this sentence alone. Color is an additional layer to black and white. Then he contrasts white against green – one more layer than muted colors. The use of the word bright is yet another layer. It brings an extra sharpness to the picture.

"Let's move on to his second sentence: 'Then…I see the ball going there; its path, trajectory and shape, even its behavior on landing.'

"Again, if you ask people how the ball would get to where they want it to go, most of their answers wouldn't be very descriptive. They'd probably draw a line from point A to point B. However, the three-dimensional description Nicklaus gives us adds extra layers of interest to the picture. He describes trajectory, shape and motion. Greg Norman had his own variation on the technique. He would look for a tree or another background object. Then he would trace how high he wanted his ball to fly, measuring it against the tree. That exercise helped crystallize the picture of the shot in his mind.

"There's a valuable lesson to learn from Norman's approach," Doc stated. "Instead of thinking that you need to copy another person's pictures exactly, you'll probably find that the more you play with these ideas, the more likely you are to develop your own style.

"Up to this point we've looked at examples of layering the sense of vision only, but there are other senses you should work with. For instance, do you think you could associate sound with hitting a golf ball?"

"Of course, Doc," Jason answered. "There's sound when the ball clicks off the club face and when it whistles through the air. It even makes some kind of sound when it hits the ground again – probably something like a thud."

"Excellent," Doc nodded. "So what you want to do is imagine the correct sounds before you swing, so that your body moves in ways that complement how you want the shot to turn out. Let's look at another sense. Could you experience the sense of touch?"

"Yeah," Jason replied again. "We talked about this in the car on the way home from your place last time. We could feel the vibration of the club when we make contact with the ball. Or, maybe we could be aware of the texture of the grip, but that has to be the limit, right, Doc? I can see applying touch and sound to our pictures, but there's no way we can apply taste and smell, is there?"

"Yes and no," answered Doc. "It's true that you can't taste or smell your shots, but there is value in fudging the senses. By associating the taste of something you ate, or the scent of the flowers on the course where you hit an especially successful shot, you can create a richer picture of that particular shot.[53]

"You could call this the Einstein factor, because it's an intelligent way of applying more information to the equation. The more descriptive you can make your pictures, and the more senses you involve, the more vivid they'll become."

Doc could see the men were thinking about associations that would make their pictures more vivid, so he paused for a moment. "Okay, have you had enough time? Good. Let's look at Nicklaus's third scene: '… the next scene shows me making the kind of swing that will turn the previous images into reality.'

"Just seeing yourself making the correct motion, as Nicklaus describes it, is a good thing to do. However, you can take this image a step further. What mood are you in when making a swing? Are you anxious, rushed, tense, frustrated? Maybe you're passive, even lethargic, or bored. Would it be better to be relaxed or determined? There are dozens of possible moods. By describing the mood you want to be in when you make a swing, you increase your control over the outcome, and decrease the chance that a counterproductive mood will affect your performance.

"Possibly you'd like to describe your third picture in a way that shows you making a calm and confident swing. You might say to yourself: 'I'm as calm as a glassy lake on a still day.'"

"Pretty smooth there, Doc!" said Frank. "When I hear you go through this explanation I see there are lots of ways to improve our visualizing and imagining. Obviously it would be a good idea to start paying attention to the pictures in our minds and use the Comparing and Layering techniques you talked about to embellish them."

"Yes, it would, and it's always helpful to remember that your three pictures should be like Nicklaus's. Which of those, Frank, do you think you need to work on most? Would it be the picture of your goal, the picture of your plan, or the picture of yourself succeeding?"

"The way I see it, it's a toss up between my goal picture and my success picture. Tell me if you think I'm on the right track, Doc. In my goal picture I see the number I want my handicap to be, written beside my name on a pale green handicap card. The ink is blue and the letters are formed in the block printing style that Robbie Owen uses when he fills out our cards."

"Excellent, Frank."

"Just a second, Doc. I've got one more. In my success picture, I feel the emotional satisfaction of having a lower handicap again. My walk has a bit of a swagger to it and I have the energy I used to have when I knew I was making progress."

"I like those pictures, Frank. You could also enhance the picture of your plan with some sensory association. When you hit practice putts in the morning before your round, there will be dew on the ball. Take time to notice the drops of water on your fingers when you pick the ball up. You could see yourself after the round, sweating in the sun as you experiment with different lies in a bunker. Imagine taking a drink of lemon water. Tying these sensations to your practice will enhance the notion that you will carry them out. In the end you will see that all of your pictures are important, and refining each of them will pay off."

Doc stood up to leave the table. "Now, if you'll allow me, there's a picture I'd like to have. We're getting near the end of our lessons, fellows, so I want a memento of our time together. Excuse me for a minute while I get my camera. I'll be right back."

True to his word, Doc returned in less than a minute with his camera and a small package. "Sorry, guys, the batteries are dead. Give me a second here while I sit down and replace them with some new ones."

"You know," Kip said, as Doc occupied himself with the batteries, "I've been mulling over today's lesson and I think you've painted yourself into a corner without a door. During all of the lessons so far, you've given us examples of how the fundamentals of success apply to real life. I've appreciated that because it's allowed me to refine my golf skills even when I'm busy doing something else, away from the course. But today's lesson seems specifically designed for golf. Can we really apply this lesson to our everyday lives?"

Doc looked up. "Oh, sure you can. I haven't given you as many examples as usual because it's time for you to stand on your own. If you think hard enough, though, you'll notice your mental pictures affect all of your achievements, whether you're an athlete, a lawyer or a parent. We all grow into the pictures we create for ourselves and if you think about it, you'll see that those pictures either limit your potential, or make it boundless.

"That being said," Doc added, "you're in for a pretty exciting time. The skills you've been developing have been laying the groundwork for future peak performances. That's why our next lesson is about getting into the zone, the ultimate way to play. In fact, the lesson on getting into the zone will also require you to be more independent. We can talk about it all we want, but to truly understand zone performances, you'll have to take the time to experience the lesson yourself, in real life." Doc pushed aside the old batteries and the empty package. "Okay, I'm all set. Let's get that keepsake I was looking for."

Doc got up from his chair, walked a few feet away and aimed his camera at the Saturday morning foursome. "No, that'll never do," he said, then walked a few steps to his left for a different angle and aimed again. A moment after he raised the camera he looked up into the sky. "Now the sun's in the way." Doc moved to a third location and put a hand on his hip, studying the situation. "Now I don't have the background I want."

"Doc, you're going about this all wrong," advised Frank. "You'll never get a good picture of us if we're sitting here, around the table. We should be standing together, shoulder to shoulder."

"I just want a picture of you seated at the table, the way you normally are," Doc protested.

"Sure, and at least one of us would have our back to you," said Frank. "Don't you know anything about photography? You're supposed to compose the picture. Come on, guys," he said impatiently, "let's all go over there and use the trees as a backdrop. The lighting angle is better too."

Frank started ushering the men to a better location but had walked only three steps when he stopped. Shaking his head, he turned back toward Doc. "You set us up, didn't you? There never was going to be a picture of us at the table. You knew we'd want to pose. This is just your way of showing us that arranging ourselves for a photo and composing our mental pictures are exactly the same thing. If we play around a bit, we'll get both pictures to look just right, won't we?"

Doc smiled. As a matter of fact, he smiled like, well, like a parent watching his child discover his belly button for the first time.

The men walked to a suitable spot and each put his best face forward. Andy tucked in his shirt, Kip ran his fingers through his disheveled hair, Frank straightened his shoulders and Jason took off his baseball cap.

"Just a moment now…let me focus…There we are."

Click.

"Now, that's a great picture!"

CHAPTER 12

———————— ⬤ ————————

THE ZONE

August is a high point in the world of golf. Traditionally, professionals play the last of the majors, the PGA, in this month, and the U.S. Amateur is held toward the end of it. It was quite fitting, then, that Doc's final lesson for the Saturday morning foursome took place early in August too.

"Has everyone memorized their lines?" Frank asked once the men were on their way from the River Bend parking lot.

"Got it, buddy," said Andy. "I can't wait to see the look on Doc's face when he finds out we already know what he's going to tell us. He'll be surprised."

During the previous eight sessions, the men had enjoyed listening to Doc as he laid out the techniques designed to improve their mental skills. For this final session, they thought they would have a little fun by stealing Doc's thunder before he got started. More than that, however, they wanted to show Doc that they were taking responsibility for their own development. After all, the lessons were just about over, and in the future it would be up to the men to apply the ideas they had learned.

So even though Doc hadn't asked them to, they had looked

into the topic of zone experiences and the work of key psychologists in the field. One of them was Dr. Mihaly Csikszentmihalyi, also known as the Guru of Flow. Over the course of more than 8,000 interviews, he had found that there are eight characteristics commonly reported by people who have had zone or flow experiences. Knowing that Doc was sure to work those points into his lesson, the men decided to memorize two characteristics each and be prepared to recite them before Doc got into the discussion.

"That professor with the funny name really knows his stuff, doesn't he?" mused Jason during the short ride.

"Hey, he's studied flow for more than 35 years. He should know what he's talking about," said Frank.

"You know what, Frank? This terminology is doing it to me again. Some people call it flow and some call it the zone. Do you think those two words mean the same thing?" Kip wondered.

"Well, did you notice that our professor friend found the characteristics he discovered not only applied to athletic performance, but also to life in general? When I read his material I thought of the zone as a peak performance in sports, and flow as a higher quality of everyday life. I know none of the researchers divide it up that way, but it was easier for me to understand the ideas looking at it like that."

"Yeah. That works for me too."

• • •

Soon the Saturday morning foursome had reached Doc's house and piled out of the car for their last official lesson.

"Hey, Doc," said Kip, greeting the man who had become their mentor and friend over the course of the summer. "I'm really looking forward to what you have to say today. Even though I've touched what I think is the edge of the zone a couple of times myself, I often hear people talk about floating along and having every shot turn out just the way they want. That would be neat. And I sure could use a peak performance in the Amateur in a week or so."

"Kip, I'm not so sure that your image of floating along once you've entered the zone is very accurate," said Doc. "The exhilaration people report from a zone experience usually comes after it's over. When you're in the process it's always intense and often even a gut-wrenching experience.[54] That's because without stretching yourself nearly to the breaking point, it's not possible to rise to a higher level. And without that stress and strain there can be no release. I'm not trying to scare you, but getting into the zone requires the willingness to push yourself to the limit.

"As for entering into the zone, no one has ever proved you can achieve it on demand. However, there are ways of knocking on the door. It only stands to reason that if you knock often enough it'll open for you at least once in a while. It also helps to know that **there are specific characteristics of zone experiences**. By developing the skills consistent with these characteristics, which is what our lessons have been about all along, you will not only increase how often you get into the zone, but how long you stay there each time."

"I wonder," said Jason, "would one of those characteristics be that we need to have really, really **clear goals?** Not just overall goals, but immediate goals, too, telling us from minute to minute what we need to do? If we did, and paid close attention to how we're doing, the **feedback** would help us build to a peak experience, wouldn't it?"

"Smart observation," Doc began.

"Hey, I know," Kip interrupted. "I bet an important key is to **match challenges to abilities.** The challenges should be big enough to keep us keen, and make us stretch, but not so big that we fall flat on our face trying. Also, we should **lose self-consciousness,** so we're not so boxed in by our self-image."

"As a matter of fact..." Doc started to say.

"You know what?" cut in Andy. "One of the characteristics is probably **control of mind and body.** Tiger always says he just focuses on what he can control, instead of outside influences. And I bet a person has to be **totally absorbed** in what he's doing. Tiger's amazing that way. As a matter of fact, Tiger reminds me a lot of myself when it comes to those two things!"

By now, Doc had figured out what the men were doing, so he sat back and listened to Frank's finishing effort.

"One thing I know for sure, when you're in the zone, your **concentration and focus** are razor sharp. It's probably because you're paying attention to every little detail. But I tell you, you really know you've been in the zone when **time becomes distorted.** It might pass quickly, or it might pass slowly. Either way, time distortion is a giveaway that you've had a special experience."

Doc raised his hands in surrender. "Okay, okay. I know when I've been had. You've listed the eight characteristics that Mihaly Csikszentmihalyi says are common to flow experiences.[55] I was going to explain them, but you must have looked into his work already."

"We thought we'd show off for you, Doc," Frank said proudly, "but actually I hope those characteristics aren't all there is to this lesson. We'd still like to hear your spin on all of this."

"You might be surprised at how little I have to say," replied Doc. "There's certainly more to getting into flow or the zone than simply knowing the characteristics. But really all you have to do is get one of them started. Once you do, each condition will advance the others, the way one harnessed horse helps move the whole team along. They're all connected."

"Oh, I agree totally!" Kip said exaggerating his tone just enough to let Doc know he really hadn't grasped the idea. "When I was reading what that professor guy said, I was thinking the very same thing."

"Professor guy? You mean Csikszentmihalyi?"

"Yeah, that's it. How the heck do you pronounce his name, anyway, Doc? I read his work, but his name just looks like a bunch of jumbled letters to me."

Doc laughed out loud. "Csikszentmihalyi! It's a Hungarian name pronounced Chicks-Sent-Me-High. Just say it a syllable at a time. Come on, try it." Doc repeated the name again, this time slower and more distinctly. "CHICKS-SENT-ME-HIGH."

"Oh, no problem. I can say that. Chicks…Chicks-Sent-Me…," ventured Kip.

"Go on. You've almost got it," Doc encouraged.

"Chicks-Sent-Me-High. Chicks-Sent-Me-High!"

"There you go. Perfect!"

Repeating the name a few more times, Kip enjoyed the way this complicated name began rolling off his tongue. "Does that mean I'm fluent in Hungarian now, Doc?"

"Not quite, although I bet you had a small sense of satisfaction as you learned to say his name, didn't you? And therein lies the elusive key to getting into the zone."

Four faces looked expectantly at Doc. Surely it couldn't be as simple as this. There had to be more. "Oh come on, Doc. You can't be serious that a little thing like saying a few syllables is all it takes to get into the zone," said Kip.

"In itself it isn't," Doc answered, "but finding a way to create any success – even one as small as pronouncing a new name – and then building on that success is at the heart of all achievement. Many people think they need to do something sensational to get them going, but usually the start is much more basic. In fact, if you **practice finding your smallest unit of success each day** and proceed from there, you'll have more than your share of zone experiences.

"If you want," Doc added, "there's research from many other people we could discuss, but at the end of the day we'd come to the same conclusion. **Peak performance is all about incremental goals, matched to ability, in order to create a string of successes. Choosing a challenging task that you can handle, and getting started, pretty much sums up the proper approach to readying yourself for a zone experience. Do that and the door will open occasionally. When it does, do more of the same."** Then Doc sat back in his chair, signifying he had said all he wanted to say.

"But…but, Doc," sputtered Kip, "what about…"

Doc shrugged his shoulders. "If there are questions we haven't covered, you'll be able to answer them yourself with the skills you've developed. When applied, those skills will start a flood of successes. In our lessons, you've learned how to set goals and you've learned how to break them down into bite-sized pieces to make them clear. The smaller and more specific the goals, the more likely you'll notice the feedback that'll keep you on track. Should you lose your way, your ability to encourage yourself and ask quality questions will help you refocus on your objective. If you need fresh input, reverting to your childlike learning skills will help you absorb what you need.

"There's no doubt that from this point on, you're going to accomplish much more than you ever thought possible. All you need to do now is find a road to travel down so you can display your talents. We all know people who have tremendous talent but never apply it to something of consequence, possibly because they never learned how easy it is. That's a shame.

"But I guess that's not a problem for you, is it, Kip? All along you've had a goal of traveling the road to the Masters with the U.S. Amateur as a stop along the way. The Amateur is an excellent opportunity to put all of the ideas we've talked about to the acid test. And speaking of that tournament, I've been meaning to ask you for some details. Could you fill me in on your plans? My schedule opens up around that time and I've been planning to go over to watch you play."

"Doc," said Kip, "that would mean an awful lot to me. I feel like I have a chance to do very well in the Amateur and I'd like to be able to share whatever success I have with you. Jason's caddying for me, and Frank and Andy and my family are going for sure. If things heat up a bit, a group of my buddies from around here will show up too. They all have directions and information on accommodations, so I really hope you're able to make it."

"Oh, I'll be there alright. There's nothing I'd rather do," said Doc.

• • •

As Kip, Jason, Andy and Frank left Doc's house later that evening, they experienced a variety of emotions. They would miss the routine of meeting with Doc, but knew they had developed a long-term relationship with him, and besides, he was only a phone call away if they needed friendly advice. They were also enthused about their success. Under Doc's tutelage, Frank had lowered his handicap by three strokes, a month ahead of his September 20th target for a two-stroke improvement, but for him, the bigger success was that he'd been rejuvenated. That's because he developed a new approach to the game. Instead of spending all his time trying to acquire a repetitive version of his imperfect golf swing, Frank took what he had learned from Doc to explore the boundaries. On the range he alternately hit shots with one hand, from a two-foot-high tee, and backward with the club turned upside down. He asked other players what their visual images were and tried some of them out. He even played a round of golf left-handed just to see what it was like. The mental elasticity gained from these and other experiments actually made him more receptive to, and capable of, making swing improvements. But he was hardly surprised. Nothing he learned from Doc surprised him anymore.

Incredibly, Andy had learned something about learning. In the past, he had flitted from one 'swing secret' to another, never really giving any skill a chance to develop properly. For instance, he had heard the story about how Nicklaus pictured his shots and he had even tried it once for two full holes! After Doc's lesson, he tried it out again and realized he actually had been making subtle, yet effective, progress with the technique each time he visited it. He came to understand that a person doesn't integrate everything about a new fundamental in one day. Granted, Andy's outward progress wasn't as dramatic as that of the other three men, but his new understanding was a good starting point. As for the 11th green, believe it or not, later in the season Andy drove a ball onto the fringe. That made him happy.

Jason's progress was significant too. Many older members at the club thought his achievements were a result of his physical coming of age. However, that theory didn't account for the fact that Jason had improved faster than other golfers in his peer group who were growing just as much. Jason noticed that every time he made some mental progress, his physical skills had more room to grow. His mental skills would then leapfrog his physical abilities, bringing him to another new level. Jason knew this two-pronged progress would allow his developing abilities to grow into all that they could be. Nothing would be stifled. So, instead of hoping that someday he would play the PGA tour, Jason was certain he had found a formula that gave him the best chance of getting there.

And Kip? Well, Kip became the biggest beneficiary of all.

• • •

Six feet two inches. The television announcers knew the distance. They had already broadcasted the information across North America and to every golf community around the world. Kip also knew the distance. U.S. Amateur officials had used a tape measure to determine how far Kip's ball was from the hole, and that his opponent would putt first because the latter's ball was half an inch further away. This was the last hole of regulation play in the U.S. Amateur final, and the contestants had been tied going into it. Now, however, one of them was putting for a possible tie, the other for a win.

Kip handed his ball to Jason for a routine cleaning and the two of them stepped aside while Kip's opponent took his turn. The large gallery surrounding the 18th green included the familiar faces of Kip's friends and family. Doc, Andy and Frank were among them, perfectly positioned to view the drama.

Kip looked directly at his friends but didn't register the image. He was too busy working out how he was going to handle his next challenge. Noticing Kip's preoccupation, Doc, Frank and Andy looked at each other and silently communicated their awareness of Kip's concentration.

It also crossed their minds that Kip had hurdled a fantastic set of challenges to get to this point. The historical records of the U.S. Amateur would show in black and white that Kip Raston was a finalist in this championship, but it wouldn't tell the story of the colorful experiences that had brought him here.

With Jason along to caddy, Kip had arrived at the tournament site the previous Saturday to play his practice rounds. A 36-hole Monday/Tuesday stroke-play qualifier followed, providing the opportunity for 64 of the 312 sectional qualifiers to advance to the match-play portion of the U.S. Amateur Championship. Kip shot 67-71, 4 under par for that stretch, and earned a berth.

Match play is a different type of competition than the more common stroke play. Instead of winning a tournament over three or four rounds based on having the lowest score, players advance one round, and one opponent, at a time. The victor at the end of each round is the player who beats his opponent on more holes than his opponent beats him. Win, and the player advances to play another round. Lose, and the player is out of the tournament. The eventual champion is the player who wins six matches scheduled between Wednesday and Sunday.

All of the matches during the week had been exciting, with some more notable than others. Warming up for his match on Wednesday, Kip noticed his swing didn't feel quite right, so he immediately decided on a specific, and extremely small, goal. He would start out just aiming for conservative target areas instead of attempting perfect shots. The minor success of parring the first two holes gave Kip the confidence that he could find a way to play well, even if he didn't feel in top form. That was very satisfying, and Jason noticed Kip's demeanor become relaxed as a result.

As success and confidence fueled each other, Kip raised the bar ever so slightly, trying to hit more specific areas and shaping his shots more exactly. By the time he got to the 18th hole of that tightly contested match, he was firing at flags tucked into corners of the greens.[56] Later, when he reflected on what he had learned in his opening win, Kip realized his smallest-unit-of-success strategy had been the key. Smaller goals meant better feedback because there were fewer variables to interfere with the message. The mini-zone he experienced over the last nine holes was the first of more, and lengthier, zone experiences to come that week.

Thursday morning, Kip nearly waited too long to learn his next lesson. When he got to the first tee, the previous day's idea of starting out hitting manageable target areas seemed like a waste of time. Admittedly, the strategy of matching challenge to ability had worked Wednesday, but hadn't he proven himself already? Kip decided he would pick up where he had left off – hitting precision shots.

However, in attempting to hit perfect shots right out of the gate, Kip lost his composure. Even his good shots frustrated him because they didn't seem to measure up to the previous day's best.

Kip lost the first three holes and was on his way to making a tournament exit when he finally realized his mistake. He needed to build up to a peak performance again, the same way a race car needs to pick up momentum before it can reach full speed, each and every time it's wheeled out onto the track. So he got to work on the par-5 fourth hole by setting a goal of just hitting the fairway, even if it meant giving up a few yards.[57] Despite his best effort, the ball trickled into the first cut of rough. In times past, Kip might have been exasperated, but by being patient he allowed that shot to be the turning point in the match. He methodically positioned his second shot properly for an optimum angle into the green, setting up an approach shot that gave him a good chance at a birdie. Kip was back in the groove.

Sticking with the plan, Kip steadily made up ground until he erased his early deficit, and won the match on the first extra hole. He was not only happy with the victory, but also with the very important lesson he learned. To reach a mountain peak a second time, you must start with small increments of success a second time. The increments may be different from day to day, yet they must still be small. He kept that in mind as he claimed his second win of the day that afternoon and third overall in the tournament.

Kip played very well on Friday. Having hit his stride, momentum carried him through the day with another solid win. Suddenly, he was heading into Saturday and the biggest opportunity of his golfing career. With only four men remaining in the tournament, the field would be narrowed to two finalists at the end of the day. Two very special finalists. They were the competitors who traditionally received an invitation to play in the Masters the following spring. As an amateur, it was Kip's best opportunity to realize his earlier dream of walking the fairways of Augusta, shoulder to shoulder, with the likes of Tiger Woods, Vijay Singh and Adam Scott.

Kip woke up at 7 a.m. on Saturday morning after a restless night. He showered in a daze and got dressed. Joining Jason for breakfast, Kip didn't even taste the food that passed his lips. His mind was racing with the enormity of the task before him. His semifinal match would be televised that day, he had the opportunity to earn an invitation to the Masters and he was only one win away from playing for his first national title. In the past, he'd reached similar critical points and failed to perform as well as he wanted to. The Willow Park Invitation and the sectional qualifier earlier this year were such occasions. In those events, thoughts of what his performance meant would start hammering at his skull and the same thing was happening now. Kip was in trouble and he knew it.

Back in his room after breakfast, Kip quickly dug out his copy of Tiger Woods's book *How I Play Golf.* Searching through a section about Tiger's mental approach, he came across something that hit home.

On three successive pages, talking about three different conditions, Tiger wrote one consistent sentence: "I focus only on what I can control."[58] Kip was determined, then and there, to use the same approach for the challenges of the day.

Kip's first challenge – his anxiety level – was an internal situation and there were two things affecting it that he could control. First, he used the body-talk and self-talk skills he had learned during the lessons with Doc to calm down as best he could. Then he got busy with the practical things he needed to do to prepare for the day. By the time he got into his car with Jason for their trip to the golf course, Kip was much calmer and looking forward to going through his warm-up routine.

His second challenge came from an external situation. The weather all week had been in the 90s, and today's forecast was for even hotter and more humid weather. It would break the 100-degree mark. Kip didn't like extremely hot weather and, in the past, hadn't always performed well in such conditions. Yet the temperature wasn't something he could control, and there was absolutely no point in worrying about it. What he could control was his reaction to it and his preparation for it. That's why he had changed into his lightest-colored clothing and packed a few extra gloves before he left the hotel room. He also asked Jason to carry more water than usual so neither of them would become dehydrated. Small details, but if they were significant enough for Tiger to pay attention to,[59] then they were significant enough for Kip.

His third challenge appeared out of nowhere. On the second hole of the match, Kip hit a shot that seemed to be heading for the center of the green when something unexpected happened. The ball hit a greenside sprinkler-head, bounced sideways down an incline, and found its way into a small bush. The lie was unplayable. Was it bad luck? Did he deserve such a severe penalty for an otherwise good shot? The answers were immaterial. Kip refocused immediately by asking himself a different question: "How would Tiger handle this situation?" The answer was obvious. Tiger wouldn't waste one second of mental energy on something he couldn't do anything about. His job now was to take a penalty for an unplayable lie, and do the best he could with the shot he had left.

By taking control of what he could, and giving up control of external forces, Kip's self-control rose to the level of precision he needed for the match. Eventually, a routine par on the 17th hole was all Kip needed to close out his opponent and fulfill a dream. Kip was going to the Masters. He had scaled a mountain.

"HOOOOOHA!" Back at the hotel room – a room transformed into Celebration Central by Kip's parents, his brother, a sister and some friends from Aurora – Kip took the lid off of his emotions. "The Masters! I'm going to the Masters! AAAAAAAAAAHHHHH. CAN YOU BELIEVE IT?"

Bear hugs and high fives all around continued until the excitement subsided to a manageable level. Reveling in the victory, the celebrants took turns recounting their favorite shots of the match. There were a couple of long putts, a few pinpoint iron shots, and an especially great recovery. Kip, and his friends, were relieved, excited, tired, and in a mood to whoop it up all at the same time. After a while, Frank suggested that Kip had achieved his goal. "No matter what happens tomorrow, you'll always be able to say you set a goal and reached it," he said.

Holding his head in his hands as if it was going to explode, Kip countered with a combination of barely manageable excitement and reason. "I don't know what to think, Frank. I'm going to the Masters, which was a huge goal of mine. WOW! But now that I've pulled it off, where do I go from here? How do I muster enough energy for tomorrow, Doc? What do I need to do to rev up the engines again, and still keep them under control?"

"What you're doing right now is perfect, Kip," Doc advised. "You owe it to yourself to enjoy the taste of today's victory. Just remember, though, that this victory, or any other, doesn't define who you are."

"What do you mean? This is the peak of my career. Even if I don't win tomorrow, it'll always be a feather in my cap."

"Yes, it will, but what I mean, Kip, is that if you associate a picture of today's achievement too strongly with who you are, your success may trap you. It's the reverse of the mistake people make when they assign a value to themselves for a failure. In both cases, the picture of the event, frozen in time, halts your development. I don't know how much potential you have, and truthfully, neither do you. So your objective should be to stay in motion by continually matching your skills to your challenges. Enjoy yourself this evening, but tomorrow go out and bite off just enough challenge to stretch your skills, just like you've been doing all week. Not only will that approach make you a winner regardless of the outcome, it'll give you the best chance of winning the match itself."

• • •

Sunday at the U.S. Amateur is much more than just another day of competition. On each previous day there are winners and losers, but no permanent satisfaction. Every victory simply means another grueling opportunity for a player at the top of his game to match his talent against the next equally determined competitor in the draw. However, Sunday the thrill of victory is final since one contestant is destined to rise to golf celebrity status. It's no wonder then, that when the participants arrived at the course in the morning, the air was electric with anticipation.

Doc's advice the night before had been for Kip to treat this match the same way he had approached the others that week. It was sound advice despite the heightened importance of the occasion, and offered Kip a game plan he was comfortable with. Unfortunately, his game just didn't seem to want to come together.

Kip started out reasonably well, going par, birdie, bogey over the first three holes. His opponent however, started off birdie, birdie, par, for a two-up lead right out of the gate. Battling as best he could against both a difficult course and a tough competitor, Kip made great scrambling pars to halve number four and five before a routine par on number six against his opponent's bogey. Now he was only one down and the match remained that way when the next five holes were halved. The few times Kip did gain an advantage in that stretch, he either missed converting an opportunity or his opponent made an unexpected recovery.

On number 12 Kip pulled off a great shot from a downhill lie in a bunker only to have his opponent make a 35-footer to push Kip's deficit back to two. He was trying, but Kip seemed to be forcing his game, while his opponent looked to be in free flow, making shots easily and not worrying when one of them didn't come off.

Fortunately, Kip won the 13th hole when his opponent hit his tee shot out of bounds and didn't even play out. Holes 14, 15 and 16 were uneventful and Kip felt that he was in a good position being only one down with two holes to go before lunch. Then he watched as his opponent hit an iron shot to a foot-and-a-half for a win on number 17. Two down once more. Still determined to keep the match close, Kip came to the reachable par-5 18th hole with the hopes of a possible eagle or at least a birdie. But it was not to be. Kip skied his drive about 235 yards in what could only be described as a pop-up for a player of his talent. That prevented him from trying to reach the green in two, since it was guarded by water. Then, attempting to make up for his mistake, Kip tried to get too cute with his third, left it in long grass on the bank of the hazard, and made bogey. Meanwhile, his opponent had driven his ball into a better position and hit the green in regulation, winning the hole with an easy par. Three down. Kip was out of sorts and his momentum was headed in the wrong direction as the contestants broke for lunch.

Earlier, Kip had obtained clubhouse passes for his parents and friends so they could join him and Jason for lunch. Kip especially welcomed Doc's company because it was an opportunity to huddle for a review of the morning round and plan a strategy for the afternoon.

"Doc," Kip said, "I tried as hard as I could out there this morning, but I just wasn't sharp. I don't see what the problem is either. I tried using all the swing keys I've used throughout the week but nothing came together. I'm wondering what I have to do to turn this around."

"He's right, Doc," said Jason. "I know Kip's game pretty well, and to me he seemed to be out of rhythm. Another thing is that Kip hit shots he doesn't usually hit. He pulled a shot on number three, came right back and pushed one on number four, and I don't know where the heck that pop-up on 18 came from. It's not like him to make mistakes like that. We're going to have to find a way to get rid of those kinds of shots if he wants to get back into this match."

"Well you know, guys," Doc said calmly, "we all hit poor shots, but the only truly disastrous ones are those you don't get feedback from. The really wayward shots you hit out there today, Kip, are your swing's way of trying to tell you something. When you hit shots that are so out of character for your game that you hardly recognize them, it's not necessarily because you're thinking of the wrong thing. It's most likely you're thinking of too many things. If you want to play your best, you need to think less. So when you're looking for a swing key, which is simply a process goal, finding the right key is less important than finding fewer keys."[60]

Kip sat back in his chair and looked at Doc for a while. "Hmmm. I guess you're saying less is more. That's interesting. You're right, though. I know that the times I've played my best, especially this week, I've thought about almost nothing. I was probably doing what you're suggesting without even realizing it."

"You probably were," said Doc. "There's no magic swing key, however. Just pick one you like. That key won't suit everyone and will even be different for each individual from day to day. If the one you select doesn't suit you, look for another until you find one that works. Then ride it for all it's worth."

"Well then, you know what I'm going to do this afternoon?" said Kip. "I'm just going to work on hitting the ball on the center of the club face. I've always liked the feel at impact when the ball hits the sweet spot no matter what club I'm swinging. I hardly have to think of anything else and my swing is right there."

"Great idea, Kip. That'll certainly provide you with excellent feedback, and an opportunity to fight your way back into this match."

"I think so too," nodded Kip, looking at his watch. "Let's get going, Jason. We've got to get out and hit a few shots, roll a few putts and be ready to tee off in 40 minutes."

Kip got feedback on the very first shot he hit in the afternoon round. The trouble was it wasn't the kind he was looking for. The first hole at this parkland course, the 19th of the contest, was a slight dogleg left par 4 and Kip pulled his tee shot. He thought he had worked out his problems on the practice range but the interfering thoughts from too many other swing keys didn't want to go away until they were purged under game conditions. Immediately after making the swing, Kip knew what he had done wrong and he was steamed at himself for letting his naturally flowing swing get so far off track.

The shot he now faced was from a side-hill, up-hill lie in heavy grass about 110 yards from the green, right behind a maple in the prime of its life. Kip walked up behind his ball, stuck his hands on his hips and looked over the prospects. The tree stared back at him, defending access to the target like a bloated goalie. People in the gallery shook their heads. Chipping out sideways or backward to the fairway was all they could envision.

"What do you think Jason? Can I get the ball over the top of that tree?" Kip asked crisply.

"You might if you can get enough club on the ball," answered Jason. "The slope means you'll have to swing the club like a base-ball bat. You probably need more club."

Kip took a pitching wedge from the bag and set it behind the ball. As soon as he did, he could feel that this setup would cause the ball to be pulled left of the target because of the side-hill lie. He opened the club face and could picture the ball traveling on line, but knew that such a lofted club wouldn't carry the ball all the way to the pin.

Kip walked back to Jason, exchanged the wedge for a nine-iron and returned to the ball. Adjusting his setup in a variety of ways, Kip's vision of the shot grew incrementally as he listened to the feedback every trial adjustment provided him. He positioned the ball further back in his stance, and then further forward. He moved his hands higher, then lower, and then higher again. As he became involved in the process of the challenge, the disappointment he had felt after his tee shot gave way to the excited anticipation of pulling off the shot.

It was the same primal feeling he had experienced time and again when he was a youngster inventing trick shots in competition with his friends at River Bend. "Hey, let's see who can hit it under that branch." "Put the ball real close to that trash can and try to hit it over." "How about this? You put my ball in a bad lie and I'll put out yours in one and see who can chip it closest to the pin." Often they failed to make the shots. But when they did, their pent-up exhilaration was released with peals of innocent laughter. As Kip stood over the ball getting a feel for this shot, that precise exhilaration entered his body.

Taking the club back, Kip swung as rhythmically as he could and made contact. The impact of the ball reverberated up the shaft into his hands, while the click on the club face traveled through the air to his ears. He knew from those sensations exactly where the ball was going. It rose steadily against the tree, skimmed by the outstretched limbs of the maple, and reached the apex of its flight a few inches above the highest leaf. Then it disappeared on its way to the ground on the other side. Losing sight of the ball, Kip quickly scampered up the slope and into the fairway so he could see around the tree. Those in the gallery who could move fast enough followed in his wake. Kip's effort was rewarded with the sight of the ball landing softly on the edge of the green, rolling down a slope toward the pin and finally coming to rest about 15 feet away. The crowd gasped their approval at the amazing result and Kip strode confidently toward the green.

Doc, who had been watching from an angle that provided a view of both the ball's original spot and the pin, looked back to notice a young boy of about 10 hurry over to the place Kip had hit his shot from, after the rest of the spectators moved on. The youngster placed his feet in the soft grass exactly where Kip's had been and stretched out his thin arms to hold an imaginary club. After taking a long look at the top of the tree to gauge the challenge, the boy swung mightily and then held the pose long enough to live the moment for himself. Kip had won the heart and imagination of a fan he hadn't yet met. Doc's suspicion was that there would be many more before the day was over.

After his opponent putted and missed from 17 feet it was Kip's turn. Had he been content to ease the putt close to the hole for the half, he wouldn't have been the caliber of player who earns a spot in a U.S. Amateur final. There was no time to relax. This was the time to take his unexpected opportunity one step further. Besides, every cell in his body, intoxicated by the exhilaration his recovery shot had produced, now craved a repeat of the same adrenalin rush. Intuitively looking to satisfy that demand, Kip continued with his swing key – feeling the ball on the club face. Then, stroking the putt and finding the adrenalin fix for a second time, Kip was suddenly transformed from being worried about himself and how well he'd do in the match to enjoying the beauty of the game – simply striking a ball and watching it seek out a target. Kip became an observer, as if he was looking down on himself from 50 feet above. Watching his 15-foot putt roll true and drop into the cup, Kip found himself only two down and rejuvenated. Moments earlier he had been facing the prospect of being four down.

Charged up after winning a hole he thought he'd lose, Kip became more assertive. Instead of wondering how he would play the rest of the day, he told himself at every stage how he wanted to play. Facing a tight landing area on the next hole he said to himself, "This shot can be made. Start the ball at that tall tree and let it work back to the middle. You've got the shot. Go ahead and hit it."

The next seven holes progressed with Kip continuing to assure himself in similar small steps. "You can do it." "Hang in there." "You can get it up and down from here."

This affirmative self-talk combined with constant feedback to push the mechanics of Kip's game into the background. The result was that Kip's play got into a wonderful rhythm. He started to see shots more clearly and began to swing out toward the target with total confidence that his shots would come off as planned. So while the two competitors exchanged blows like heavyweight fighters in the form of one quality shot after another in this stretch, by the 27th hole Kip had rallied for three more birdies against one for his opponent to finally pull even in the match.

The 28th hole saw Kip lose the lead yet again to a birdie, but the 29th provided a small opening if he could just pull off a tricky chip. Kip faced a hole location cut very close to the high side of the green, requiring him to make a delicate little shot. He said to himself, "Bounce it once in the fringe to deaden the pace, and it'll trickle right down to the pin." Kip thought he may have hit the ball too hard, but the shot turned out perfectly and then he slaved over a five-footer for the win. He had drawn even again.

A beautiful six-iron that never left the flag on the par-3 30th hole gave Kip a short birdie putt and the lead for the very first time all day. A one-hole lead, however, was a minor deterrent to an opponent who had no intention of rolling over. The two contestants tied the 31st and 32nd holes before Kip's opponent rolled in a long putt for birdie on the 33rd to tie and another on 34th to take the lead back. There was no coasting. Kip would have to gear up and fight hard once again just to tie up the match. His tee shot on the 35th hole found a sand-filled divot, but Kip simply ignored the frustration. He analyzed the swing he needed to make and hit a great shot to set up his seventh birdie of the afternoon round, meaning the two players came to the last hole all even.

This time Kip's drive on the final hole was no pop-up. Flying long and straight, it left him with an opportunity to hit the par 5 in two. Walking toward his ball in the fairway Kip said something Jason didn't expect.

"You know, Jason, I should pinch myself. Here I am slugging it out with a player who's trying to beat my brains in as much as I am his. But the better he plays the more I want to rise to the challenge. I think he feels the same way too, because he's hitting some unbelievable shots. I love it, and to me this is what competition is all about. It just doesn't get any better than this."[61]

Up to then Jason had been nervous for Kip because he recognized this late stage in the game as the one where Kip's demons would typically surface. Digesting what Kip had just said about his opponent spurring him on made Jason realize that Kip had replaced those demons with a much healthier approach. He marveled at how far his buddy had come in a few short months, but said nothing. Just standing there radiating confidence was enough for Kip to notice that Jason believed he was about to pull off another critical shot.

Standing in the middle of the fairway, Kip watched his opponent hit a shot that finished slightly left of the green. It left him with a long, difficult chip to set up a chance for a birdie.

Advantage Kip. After playing catch-up most of the day, the door was now open for him to press that advantage. Instead of playing safely to the fat left-hand portion of the kidney-shaped green and leaving himself with a long breaking putt, Kip could fire at the narrower right-hand portion of the green where the pin was located. The gamble had its risks. Too long and the ball would go into heavy rough. Too short and the water hazard would seal his fate. One of Kip's skills was sound course management – the selection of high-percentage shots. Under normal conditions this wasn't one of them.

However, these weren't normal conditions. Kip's body and mind had been working in such harmony for the past three-and-a-half hours that he knew exactly how the two of them would perform now. At this moment Kip felt he was capable of making the shot.

"All I have to do," he said to himself, "is hit a high fade that carries just short of the knoll in the center of the green and let the ball feed to the right." Kip selected a four-iron from the bag and went through his routine. With a picture of the landing area riveted in his mind, Kip knew where the shot was headed as soon as it left the club face. The ball cut a path through the sky, faded slightly to the right, and tracked toward the target. When it landed, the ball kicked off the hard, fast green as envisioned and rolled toward the pin. He had gained the advantage he was looking for, but seeing where it came to rest on the slope Kip knew his job wasn't over.

Kip made the long walk to the green and marked his ball so that it wouldn't interfere with his opponent's chip. After considerable time analyzing his own difficult shot, Kip's opponent played it up about as close to the hole as Kip's ball was. Not knowing who had the honor, a USGA official was called upon to determine who was further away. A tape measure had to be used to determine that Kip's eagle putt was a mere six feet two inches from the cup. His opponent's birdie attempt was half an inch further, so he would go first.

Kip handed Jason his ball for a routine cleaning and the two of them stepped aside while Kip's opponent took his turn.

Looking straight ahead, Kip's mind didn't register the people around him but he heard the sudden noise a minute later. The knowledgeable crowd, keenly aware of the tension facing both players and the difficulty of each shot under such pressure, had let out a roar. Kip's opponent had made his putt, giving him a chance to tie should Kip miss his. Jason slapped the ball he had cleaned back into its owner's hand. It was Kip's turn to occupy center stage. He walked over to the area of the green where he had marked his ball earlier.

Looking over the putt from both sides of the hole with Jason's assistance, the difficulty of the putt was reconfirmed. His opponent had made an uphill putt, but Kip's was on a severe side-hill slope. The greens were running at 11.5 on the stimpmeter,[62] meaning that the ball, should it miss, could easily travel eight feet past the hole. In effect, Kip was looking at the possibility of winning, tying, or losing the opportunity to become the U.S. Amateur champion based on the outcome of this putt. The ideal approach was for Kip to play the ball high enough to catch the fall line and let it descend toward the hole without excessive speed. A possible error would be to hit it so softly that it would fall short or start to waver rather than roll true and hold its line. The other error would be to putt too aggressively and hit the ball through the break.

Considering the importance of the shot, it would be easy for any one of the many muscles in Kip's hands to become overanxious and ruin the normally smooth pace of his putting stroke. With multiple unsatisfactory possibilities and only one desirable outcome, Kip asked himself a question. "What do I have to do to make this putt?" Once he did, his body and mind took on the task of searching for the feel that would provide the answer.

Kip began his routine. He placed his ball in front of his marker and aligned the logo in the direction he wanted the ball to start out. With the proper direction set, he picked up the marker and placed it in his pocket. Standing back, he registered one picture in his mind of how the cup wished to receive the ball and another of his body making the stroke to match. Kip took one practice stroke to rehearse that feeling and addressed the ball before taking a last look at the hole. He took the putter back. The putter accelerated rhythmically through the ball. Out of the corner of his eye Kip knew he had sent it firmly on its way.

The ball rolled end over end, seeking a resting point. Just when it seemed to want to slip by the high side, the ball slowed down. For a portion of a second there was emptiness. There was no sound, no feedback and no reaction from the crowd. It was actually possible for everyone to calculate what was going to happen based on the speed of the ball, but it took a distorted moment in time to register the meaning. The ball disappeared. The sound it made when it hit the bottom of the cup was not a click. It was an explosion echoing the roar of every person in sight. The prize was his. Kip Raston, a regular guy who played golf with the same passion millions of other people do all across the nation, was now the U.S. Amateur Champion!

All the emotion Kip had been harnessing for a week reorganized itself inside his body, in new and different ways. As relief and exhilaration vied for expression on his face, Kip's right arm punched the sky in victory. His friends and family, the nearest spectators, raised Kip to their shoulders ahead of the crowd pressing in. When the cheers settled down to a dull roar, a television broadcaster stood at Kip's side with a microphone, ready to amplify every word uttered by golf's newest hero.

"Kip Raston. Congratulations! You must be exhausted, but can you tell the viewers how it feels to be the U.S. Amateur Champion?"

"I feel numb, just numb. Oooooooh! I can hardly believe it. I don't think I know what's happened."

"Kip, one year ago you weren't even on the national radar, and today you're on top of the world of amateur golf. What's the single most important thing that made the difference?"

Still trying to gather control of his emotions, Kip answered as best he could. "The one thing that made the biggest difference is that there wasn't one thing. It was little things – a whole bunch of little things. All week I looked for small successes and eventually I had so many of them that I guess this is where they took me. Man! This is a good feeling."

"Well, obviously your strategy worked," the interviewer said. "Anyone who had the pleasure of watching you saw a golfer who was really dialed in. And that iron shot you hit to the last green was amazing! What gave you the confidence you could trust your swing in such a pressure-packed situation?"

"Oooooooh man!" Kip exhaled, as a second realization of what he had just done washed over him. "I just saw the shot and it happened. As a matter of fact, to tell you the truth, right now I don't want to know how I did it. It's more fun just enjoying it."

"Kip, you had to know that your last putt was six feet two inches long, but there was another 6-2 in you today. You made 11 pars, seven birdies and one eagle on a par-71 golf course. Even though it's unofficial because this is match play, by my math, that adds up to a 9 under par score of 62.[63] In your wildest dreams, did you ever think you had that kind of score in you when you needed it most?"

"Sixty-two?" Kip repeated, stunned by the echo of the number. His mind went back to his first lesson with Doc as he searched for the reason. "Yeah, I knew I was on a roll, but I wasn't thinking about the actual score, especially, like you say, since we were playing head-to-head. But it's funny. At the beginning of the season, a friend of mine got me to work out a plan to shoot exactly that number. It's been sitting in the back of my mind all along and I sort of knew it would happen some day. I just don't know any other way to explain it."

"Well, you don't have any more explaining to do, Kip. Your name goes on the trophy alongside some pretty famous golfers. Two of the best to ever play the game come to mind, Nicklaus and Woods. Do you see yourself following in their footsteps?"

"Gee, I can hardly think about anything like that right now. Me and Woods? Me and Nicklaus?! Wow! I don't know, but I can tell you I'm going to do one thing they did. I'm going to keep taking the next small step, whatever it is. If you ask me… HEEEYYYYYYY!"

At that moment, a spray of champagne showered Kip, stinging his eyes and soaking his hair. Although he couldn't actually see the person who held the bottle, Kip could pretty well guess it was Andy who had popped the cork. Peering through the bubbly, he finished his thoughts.

"...If you ask me tomorrow, maybe I'll have low amateur at the Masters in the back of my mind. Overall, though, I'm going to keep my eye on whatever small improvement it makes sense for me to tackle next. I don't know exactly where it'll take me, but keeping my eye on the next rung on the ladder is what got me here, so I'm going to stick with the plan and keep on going."

"Sounds like you'll be going far, Kip. Pretty far indeed."

• • •

The interviews and celebrations were over. The last stragglers were leaving the course, and equipment was being loaded back into the media trucks. Kip and Jason were putting their belongings into their car for the return trip home. From across the parking lot, the youngster who had imitated Kip's swing on the first hole that afternoon made his way toward them with his father in tow. Approaching his hero timidly he said, "Mr. Raston, would you write your name in my book?"

Kip looked quizzically at the boy. He recognized the cover of the book he was holding, *The 3 Fundamentals of Success*, but didn't quite understand. The father of the boy spoke up. "We were in the golf shop after the match and heard that you used this book to teach yourself all about the mental game. My son, Ryan, here just can't stop talking about you so we bought a copy and I thought it would be a great keepsake if we could also get your autograph. I'm sure it's something he'd treasure forever."

Kip bent over at the waist so he could be at eye level with the young boy and signed his name, but held onto the book for a moment. "Ryan, I signed your book because you asked me to, but

I hope you realize I didn't write it. It was written by a friend of mine named Doc, who organized the experiences of lots of famous people into a story to make the lessons interesting."

The young boy shyly nodded his understanding. Happy to have his hero speak to him, he would have agreed with anything Kip said.

The boy's father, however, was intrigued. "You say you know the fellow who wrote it. If he was here, what advice do you think he'd give my son?"

As Kip considered this question, he wondered if the father was actually asking on his own behalf instead of his son's, so he stood up to address both of them at the same time. "I think Doc would say that the way we choose to think determines the person we become and our level of fulfillment in life. So regardless of how we've lived so far, if we want to progress from here on in, we would do well to imitate how great people think." Kip paused for a moment. "And personally I would say this: if you take Doc's book and write in it, you'll be the author of your own success. I did and it worked for me. If you do, it'll work for you too."

ENDNOTES

The purpose of these endnotes is not only to cite sources, but also to provide the reader with an understanding of the concepts underlying *How Great Golfers Think*. Therefore, I have quoted short amounts of text from some, but not all, sources when I felt more information would be helpful.

Also, in some cases, I have offered further clarification on a point in my own words using [bracketed text].

1. Handicap

[The highest allowable handicap under United States Golf Association guidelines, for a male golfer, is minus 36. The highest allowable for a female golfer is minus 40. This means a 36-handicap player subtracts 36 strokes from his score to equalize himself with a zero handicap golfer, often called a scratch player. A player that is better than a zero handicap needs to add strokes to his score to equalize himself with a zero handicap. Therefore, he is called a plus handicap player. Thus, Kip, at plus two, is two strokes better than Jason, at zero, and 10 strokes better than Frank, who is an eight handicap. Tour professionals commonly have handicaps of plus five or better, although such calculations are rarely recorded.]

2. Crow's Nest

John Boyette, *Amateurs Enjoy Crow's Nest's View*. The Augusta Chronicle. April 9, 2004, Augusta National. [Last accessed August 16, 2007.] http://www.augusta.com/masters2004/stories/040904/cou_557974.shtml [The Crow's Nest is the uppermost room in the Augusta National Golf Club clubhouse. In recent years, it has lodged five amateurs during the Masters – the U.S. Amateur winner and runner-up, the British Amateur champion, the U.S. Mid-Amateur winner and the U.S. Public Links champion. The location of the 30-by-40-foot room is recognizable by the 11-foot square cupola above it, and visible from outside the clubhouse.]

3. **Self-talk components**

B. S. Rushall and M. L. Shewchuck, *Effects of Thought Content Instructions on Swimming Performance.* Journal of Sports Medicine and Physical Fitness, 1989, Vol. 29, No. 4, p. 326. The effects of instructions to use three different types of thought patterns on the practice performance of superior age-group swimmers were assessed….Group averages indicated that task-relevant content was the most effective condition, followed by mood words, and positive thinking.

4. **Breaking tasks into small portions**

Chip Heath, Richard P. Larrick and George Wu, *Goals as Reference Points.* Cognitive Psychology, 1999, Vol. 38, p. 91-93. Far away from the goal, people may not feel that they are making much progress toward their goal. In turn, they may find it difficult to motivate themselves to start a task when they face a difficult goal. We call this implication of diminishing sensitivity the "starting problem"….One way to overcome the starting problem is to set subgoals. People who set subgoals are more sensitive to progress than people who focus only on their ultimate goal. Consider the effect of subgoals in the following problem: *Problem 10.* [46 subjects] Jill is a high school cross-country runner. One summer she decides to run 1000 miles over the course of the 90-day summer break. Jill thinks of this as running 330 miles a month (30 days). The first day she runs 15 miles and wakes up quite sore. Tina is also a high school cross-country runner. One summer she decides to run 1000 miles over the course of the 90-day summer break. Tina thinks of this as running 11 miles a day. The first day she runs 15 miles and wakes up quite sore. Who is more likely to reach her overall goal for the summer? Please circle one: Jill (22%) Tina (78%)….By dividing the monthly goal into daily subgoals, Tina is better able to see progress relative to her goal. [Jill may find it difficult to motivate herself at all since her effort seems to have contributed so little to her more distant goal of 330 miles a month.]

5. Know what you want right out of the gate

E. A. Locke, K. N. Shaw, L.M. Saari and G. P. Latham, *Goal Setting and Task Performance: 1969-1980.* Psychological Bulletin, 1981, Vol. 90, No. 1, p. 131. Most fundamentally, goals direct attention and action….[In a study,] drivers were given feedback regarding five different dimensions of driving performance but were assigned goals with respect to only one dimension. The dimension for which a goal was assigned showed significantly more improvement than the remaining dimensions.

6. Public image

Tim Kasser and Richard M. Ryan, *Further Examining the American Dream: Differential Correlates of Intrinsic and Extrinsic Goals.* Personality and Social Psychology Bulletin, 1996, Vol. 22, No. 3, p. 280. Empirical research and organismic theories suggest that lower well-being is associated with having extrinsic goals focused on rewards or praise…in comparison to intrinsic goals congruent with inherent growth tendencies. In a sample of adult subjects (Study 1), the relative importance and efficacy of extrinsic aspirations for financial success, an appealing appearance, and social recognition were associated with lower vitality and self-actualization and more physical symptoms. Conversely, the relative importance and efficacy of intrinsic aspirations for self-acceptance, affiliation, community feeling, and physical health were associated with higher well-being and less distress.

7. Mastering tasks

J. L. Duda, *Goal Perspectives, Participation, and Persistence in Sport.* International Journal of Sports Psychology, 1989, Vol. 20, No. 1, p. 43. In particular, it is argued that an individual who is task involved, regardless of perceived ability level, will exert maximal effort, choose moderately challenging tasks, be more likely to perform up to his/her potential, and tend to persist in achievement situations.

8. Short-term goals

Gary P. Latham, and Edwin A. Locke, *Self-Regulation through Goal Setting.* Organizational Behavior and Human Decision Processes, 1991, Vol. 50, p. 237-238. Proximal vs Distal Goals…a recent study by Stock and Cervone (1990) suggests that proximal goals serve as highly effective self-regulators that affect performance in at least four ways. First, Stock and Cervone found that the assignment of a proximal goal increased the strength of the person's self-efficacy for completing the task....People who had been assigned a proximal goal in addition to the distal goal of task completion had significantly higher initial ratings of self-efficacy than did those people who only had a distal goal. Mentally "breaking down" the task appeared to make it appear to be manageable which in turn enhanced the person's perception that she was capable of performing it effectively. Second, reaching the proximal goal enhanced self-efficacy. As people attained the subgoal they became more confident of their capability to complete the task. Those people who reached the same level of performance without knowing that they had achieved a proximal goal showed no increase in their self-efficacy. Third, the attainment of the proximal goal affected self-evaluative re-actions positively. Those who achieved the proximal goal were more satisfied with their progress than were those people who either did not attain the subgoal or who had not been assigned one to attain. Finally, those people with proximal goals persisted on the task significantly longer than did those people who had not been assigned them. Stock and Cervone (1990) concluded that when individuals are uncertain of their ability to perform a complex, challenging endeavor, setting proximal goals can influence positively self-referent thought, motivation, and performance.

9. **Ability to reset your goals**
C. B. Botterill, *Goal Setting and Performance on an Endurance Task.* University of Alberta, unpublished doctoral dissertation, 1977, p. 5 and 45. Seventy-five boys (age 11-14) were pre-tested on a hand grip test endurance test, and post-tested on the same task following 1 of 5 treatments involving various combinations of the manipulated goal setting features.... Many subjects substantially exceeded their original goals and the experimenter noted that the better performers appeared to spontaneously reset their goals during testing. These subjects would achieve an original goal, appear more confident and motivated and continue in pursuit of another more difficult goal.

10. **Specific goals**
Michael Bar-Eli, Gershon Tenenbaum, Joan S. Pie, Yaacov Btesh and Asher Almog, *Effect of Goal Difficulty, Goal Specificity and Duration of Practice Time Intervals on Muscular Endurance Performance.* Journal of Sports Sciences, March

1997, Vol. 15, No. 2, p. 125. [Subjects] were randomly assigned to one of 15 conditions representing five levels of goal conditions – namely, 'do' (no goals), 'do your best', 'improve by 10%' (easy), 'improve by 20%' (difficult/realistic) and 'improve by 40%' (improbable/unattainable)....The results indicated that all specific groups performed better than all non-specific groups.

11. Specific goals

Locke, Shaw, Saari and Latham, *Goal Setting and Task Performance: 1969-1980.* p. 129. Twenty-four field experiments all found that individuals given specific, challenging goals either outperformed those trying to do their best or surpassed their own previous performance when they were not trying for specific goals.

12. Measurable goals

Edwin A. Locke and Gary P. Latham, *The Application of Goal Setting to Sports.* Sport Psychology's Today, Journal of Sport Psychology, 1985, 7, p. 207. The act of measuring performance itself often leads to spontaneous goal setting when there is no formal goal setting program (Saari & Latham, 1982). It is a truism in business that what gets measured gets done. The same phenomenon occurs in sports. The very act of taking the trouble to measure some aspect of performance implies its importance to the athlete.

13. Beauty of companions

Z. Zaleski, *Influence of a Close Relationship with a Partner: Relationships and Acting for Self-Set Goals.* European Journal of Social Psychology, 1988, Vol. 18, p. 191. [Besides being a hero or role model, a companion could simply be a person who offers support as follows:] The data were collected from 200 [subjects] involved in a close relationship [married, engaged, living together]....The data analysis (ANOVA) revealed that the high support (vs. low) was significantly related to greater effort, persistence and satisfaction. Also high emotional control was related to higher persistence and high dependence resulted in stronger satisfaction from goal-related activity. The path analysis showed that partner's support influences the goal-related activity in two ways, directly through enhancing persistence and satisfaction and indirectly by increasing individual's expectancy of successful goal attainment. [While this study is based on support from an intimate partner, it is reasonable to expect that anyone providing support would have a positive influence on another person.]

14. **Similar enough to yours**
A. Bandura, *Self-efficacy.* In V. S. Ramachaudran (Ed.), Encyclopedia of Human Behavior, New York, Academic Press, 1994, Vol. 4, p. 71-81. Perceived self-efficacy is defined as people's beliefs about their capabilities to produce designated levels of performance that exercise influence over events that affect their lives....People's beliefs about their efficacy can be developed by four main sources of influence....The second way of creating and strengthening self-beliefs of efficacy is through the vicarious experiences provided by social models. Seeing people similar to oneself succeed by sustained effort raises observers' beliefs that they too possess the capabilities [sic] master comparable activities to succeed.

15. **Benefit of two weeks between sessions**
G. Buzsaki, *Two-Stage Model of Memory Trace Formation: A Role for "Noisy" Brain States.* Neuroscience, 1989, Vol. 31, No. 3, p. 565. [Research shows that during sleep, the brain rewires itself to accommodate newly gained knowledge and stores it for future use. So knowing that learning is optimized when it's presented over enough time to include a sleep period, Doc spread out his lessons rather than offering them as one marathon session.] Our neurophysiological model of memory trace formation lends further support for the importance of the sleep process in memory consolidation and provides a possible physiological basis of the consolidation mechanism. It directly predicts that retention of a task will be significantly better if followed by a sleep episode, due to the abundance of SPW-bursts during slow wave sleep. The functions of paradoxical sleep might be to reload the hippocampus with the information of the preceding learning episode and to refresh the leading role of the initiator cells in SPW – concurrent population bursts during subsequent slow wave sleep epochs.

16. **Mini games**
Terry Orlick, *In Pursuit of Excellence: How to Win in Sport and Life Through Mental Training, Second Edition.* Champaign IL, Leisure Press, 1990, p. 73. [Alex Baumann, the 1984 double Olympic gold medalist and world record holder in swimming, has this to say about how he broke up his performances into what could be termed 'mini games':] The best way I have learned to prepare mentally for competitions is to visualize the race in my mind and to put down a split time. The splits I use in my imagery are determined by my coach and myself, for each part of the race. For example, in the 200

individual medley, splits are made up for each 50 meters because after 50 meters the stroke changes. These splits are based on training times and what we feel I'm capable of doing. In my imagery I concentrate on attaining the splits I have set out to do.

17 **Positive feedback and success**
Locke, Shaw, Saari and Latham, *Goal Setting and Task Performance: 1969-1980.* p. 135-136. Erez (1977) was the first to suggest that KR [Knowledge of Results] is a necessary condition for the goal-performance relation….The goal-performance correlation in the KR group was .60 and in the no-KR group, .01….Not only should specific, hard goals be established, but KR should be provided to show performance in relation to these goals.

18. **Baddeley stats**
Stats, PGA Tour. [Last accessed August 11, 2007.]
http://www.pgatour.com/players/02/23/71/stats/2005.html

19. **Jean Van de Velde**
[In the 1999 British Open, Jean Van de Velde of France had a three-shot lead with one hole to play. He made a triple-bogey and lost in a play-off to Paul Lawrie. His story is often cited as an example of letting a big one get away.]

20. **Plastic surgery and self-image**
Maxwell Maltz, *Psycho-Cybernetics: A New Way to Get More Living Out of Life.* Toronto, Prentice-Hall, 1960, p. 8. [Frank is relating a fictional story, very similar to the real-life situations told by Dr. Maltz, a plastic surgeon, in his landmark book. Maltz popularized our understanding of how self-image influences the realization of our potential.]

21. **Palmer learns from loss…scorecards are signed**
Arnold Palmer, *My Game and Yours.* New York, Simon & Schuster, 1983, p. 95.

22. **Nicklaus learns from loss…repair ball marks**
Jack Nicklaus, with Ken Bowden, *My Most Memorable Shots In The Majors.* Trumbull CT, GolfDigest/Tennis, Inc., 1988, p. 17.

23. Learn the lesson
Carol S. Dweck, *Self Theories: Their Role in Motivation, Personality, and Development.* Philadelphia, Psychology Press, Taylor & Francis Group, 2000, p. 16-17. In this study,...with fifth-grade students, we gave students a performance goal or a learning goal....Many students with performance goals showed a clear helpless pattern in response to difficulty. A number of them condemned their ability, and their problem-solving deteriorated....In sharp contrast, most of the students with learning goals showed a clear mastery-oriented pattern. In face of failure, they did not worry...they remained focused on the task, and they maintained their effective problem-solving strategies.

24. Using learning technique over and over
Nicklaus, *My Most Memorable Shots in the Majors.* [In this book, Nicklaus lists at least 55 lessons he learned in the majors alone.]

25. Nicklaus counting clubs
Jack Nicklaus, with Ken Bowden, *Golf My Way.* New York, Simon & Schuster, 1974, p. 38. [Frank is in good company. Jack Nicklaus and Deanne Beaman once lost an America's World Cup team match in the very same way. Nicklaus wrote:] Having Charlie's wedge in his bag brought his total to fifteen, which meant under the rules of that time that we lost every hole up to that point and were five down. Since then, I've counted my clubs on the first tee before every tournament round, plus my partner's in team events.

26. Tiger's physical fitness and diet
Tiger Woods, *How I Play Golf.* New York, Warner Books Inc., 2001, p. 275-293. [You can read details of Tiger's approach to physical fitness and diet in this reference.]

27. Take the walk
Orlick, *In Pursuit of Excellence: How to Win in Sport and Life Through Mental Training, 2nd Edition.* p. 99-103. [Orlick describes his experience with Indonesian and Chinese coaches and athletes. What Doc calls a walk through, Orlick calls simulation.] Indonesian athletes were world champions in badminton for an unprecedented number of years....They simulate every aspect of the game (for example, strategy, coming from behind, bad calls, high temperature, crowd effects), particularly for the world

championships....The Chinese are [also] masters of the art of simulation....the Chinese go a step beyond other countries....They prepare athletes to perform when fatigued and to meet specific opponents. For example some skilled Chinese athletes are trained to replicate the playing styles of opponents from other countries so they can provide simulation training for national team members.

28. The mind believes fiction
Stephanie J. Sharman, Maryanne Garry, and Carl J. Beuke, *Imagination or Exposure Causes Imagination Inflation.* American Journal of Psychology, Summer 2004, Vol. 117, No. 2, p. 27. Our results suggest that simply putting a fictitious experience into new words may cause people to become confident that the fictitious experience was real.

29. Doc uses a lot of questions
Rick Garlikov, *The Socratic Method: Teaching by Asking Instead of by Telling.* [Last accessed August 16, 2007.] http://www.garlikov.com/Soc_Meth.html [Doc's habit of using questions to communicate his ideas is based on a teaching experiment conducted by Rick Garlikov. Garlikov challenged himself to use questions only, instead of statements, to teach a class of students binary math in just 25 minutes. He demonstrates the potential we have when the right questions are asked. The experiment is even more interesting because the students are from a Grade 3 class.]

30. Learn in a ready position
Donald H. Meichenbaum and Jerry L. Deffenbacher, *Stress Inoculation Training.* The Counseling Psychologist, 1988, Vol. 16, No. 1, p. 83. As coping skills are mastered within session, attention is turned to transferring them to the external environment. Typically, this is done through graded homework assignments or in vivo sessions.

31. Arousal level
Deborah Graham and Jon Stabler, *The 8 Traits of Champion Golfers.* New York, Simon & Schuster, 1999, p. 180-181. [Using the same one-to-10 scale] we found that, if golf measures 4 to 6, other sports rate as follows:
Baseball – 3 to 7
Basketball – 4 to 8
Football – 6 to 9

Power lifting – 8 to 9
Hockey – 6 to 9
Target shooting – 2 to 3
...As a general rule, tasks that require more gross motor skills – such as your long game – require higher arousal and those that require fine motor skills – like your short game – require lower arousal....It's much less common for golfers to compete while in an underaroused state. But it does happen....We find this is fairly common with touring professionals who have been competing for more than a decade and with amateurs who have played for years with the same people on the same courses, all of whom are playing without having set clear, measurable, and motivating goals.

32. Stress Inoculation Training or SIT
D. Meichenbaum, *Stress Inoculation Training for Coping With Stressors.* The Clinical Psychologist, 1996, 49, p. 4-5. Stress Inoculation Training (SIT)....is a...form of cognitive behavioral therapy....In the initial *conceptualization phase* a collaborative relationship is established between the clients and the therapist (trainer). A Socratic-type exchange [see endnote #29 regarding the Socratic method] is used to educate clients about the nature and impact of stress....The clients are taught how to breakdown [sic] global stressors into specific short-term, intermediate and long-term coping goals.

The second phase of SIT focuses on *skills acquisition* and *rehearsal* that follows naturally from the initial conceptualization phase. The coping skills that are taught and practiced primarily in the clinic or training setting and then gradually rehearsed in vivo are tailored to the specific stressors clients may have to deal with (e.g., chronic illness, traumatic stressors, job stress, surgery, sports competition, military combat, etc.). The specific coping skills may include emotional self-regulation,...relaxation training, self-instructional training, cognitive restructuring. The final phase of *application* and *follow through* provides opportunities for the clients to apply the variety of coping skills across increasing levels of stressors....Such techniques as imagery and behavioral rehearsal, modeling, role playing, and graded in vivo exposure in the form of "personal experiments" are employed.

33. Pygmalion effect
R. Rosenthal and L. Jacobson, *Pygmalion in the Classroom.* New York, Holt, Rinehart and Winston, 1968.

34. Face life's challenges confidently
Earl Woods, with Pete McDaniel, *Training a Tiger: A Father's Guide to Raising a Winner in Both Golf and Life*. New York, Harper Collins, 1997, p. XI. Pop would remind me how important it is to prepare for life's challenges so that I could face them confidently. He would use golf to teach me about patience, integrity, honesty, and humility.

35. Hitting the ball a ton
Woods, *Training a Tiger: A Father's Guide to Raising a Winner in Both Golf and Life*. p. 19.

36. He had that unique ability
Woods, *How I Play Golf*. p. 11 of the Forward. I [Earl Woods] told him that he had that extra gear that all great athletes display and that he could call upon it at anytime.

37. Children absorb through senses
David Gettman, *Basic Montessori: Learning Activities for Under-Fives*. New York, St. Martin's Press, 1987, p. 5. For example, a baby in the living room of its home will absorb the complete and detailed actions and attitudes of mother reading, father tinkering, brother and sister playing a game, even if all these activities are going on at once.

38. Filtering out experiences
Gettman, *Basic Montessori: Learning Activities for Under-Fives*. p. 5. The absorbent mind acquires nearly any impression, simple or complex, with equal ease and accuracy. It primarily responds to human stimuli, especially the human voice, but within the full is impartial and non-selective.

39. Tiger learning to be aware
Woods, *Training a Tiger: A Father's Guide to Raising a Winner in Both Golf and Life*. p. 12-13.

40. Higher detail than the average person
Making the Connection: Legends of Golf. TSN, Aired July 11, 2007. [How many golfers would notice a small difference in the height of one flagstick versus another? Here's what Tom Watson, the winner of eight majors, replied to

interviewer David Feherty during an exhibition match at the Dundarave Golf Course in Charlottetown, P.E.I., in June 2006. Watson was asked if it was difficult to judge the yardages at the course.] When we come to a course that has different size flagsticks, when you've got seven-foot flagsticks versus an eight-footer everything is longer and it just messes...with your eyes.

41. Connecting information

Gettman, *Basic Montessori: Learning Activities for Under-Fives.* p. 11. The second stage of learning consists of repeatedly acting out connections between the absorbed phenomena, which for the young child again usually involves physical activity. This firmly bridges the absorbed phenomena that were only loosely associated in the first stage. [Endnote #42 is a continuation of this text. Reading #41 and #42 together may be helpful.]

42. Linking the information

Gettman, *Basic Montessori: Learning Activities for Under-Fives.* p. 11. Through repetition, the child explores and establishes all the different ways that the component phenomena fit together, so that in the end they are irrevocably joined. [Arguably, Tiger's variety of shots are a result of this type of exploration.]

43. Absorbing from all stimuli, including people

Marc R. Lochbaum, Paul Karoly and Daniel M. Landers, *Evidence for the Importance of Openness to Experience on Performance of a Fluid Intelligence Task by Physically Active and Inactive Participants.* Research Quarterly for Exercise and Sport, December 2002, Vol. 73, No. 4, p. 437, 438 and 442. Hierarchical regression analysis results revealed...that openness to experience was a significant predictor of fluid intellectual performance....Fluid intelligence is reflected in cognitive tests that require effortful, attention-demanding, step-by-step problem solving and reflects neurological structures....Personality structure is often viewed in terms of...[five] factors. Extraversion, neuroticism, agreeableness,...conscientiousness...[and] openness to experience....Open individuals are characterized by curiosity about both inner and outer worlds and are believed to be more willing to entertain novel ideas....Openness to experience may contribute to better intellectual performance because of the person's heightened state of receptivity to learning.

44. Penick 'birdie' story
Harvey Penick and Bud Shrake, *Harvey Penick's Little Red Book*. New York, Simon & Schuster, 1992, p. 40.

45. Valuable chance to learn
Michael Ungar, *Too Safe for Their Own Good: How Risk and Responsibility Help Teens Thrive*. Toronto, McClelland & Stewart, 2007, p. 2-3. [In this book, the author explains why the current culture of overprotecting our children can do them more harm than good.] Children...need opportunities to fail, and to fail often enough to learn how to pick themselves back up....An entire generation of children...are not being provided with the opportunities they need to learn how to navigate their way through life's challenges.

46. Preparation and inner confidence
Gettman, *Basic Montessori: Learning Activities for Under-Fives*. p. 2. [After Maria Montessori started her school she noticed] something very strange and wonderful about some of the children. Those who freely participated in the activities began to reveal a facet of childhood which Montressori had never seen before. Some of the more experienced children began to evidence a kind of inner calmness, and they were able to concentrate for very long periods of time. Not only did they quickly absorb complex skills and sophisticated knowledge they also developed a self-discipline which relieved any need for external authority.

47. Watermelon snow
Watermelon snow, Wikipedia. [Last accessed August 11, 2007.]
http://en.wikipedia.org/wiki/Snow and
http://en.wikipedia.org/wiki/Watermelon_snow

48. Nicklaus watching Palmer
Jack Nicklaus with Ken Bowden, *My Story*. New York, Simon & Schuster, 1997, p. 83. As I came off the course one day in heavy rain, I noticed a golfer out on the range all by himself beating balls with a short iron. I went and stood under a tree and watched him [Palmer] for probably an hour. I could hear the balls crack off the clubface, as Gary Player always described it, like thunderclaps.

49. Nicklaus seeing his swing
Nicklaus, *Golf My Way*. p. 79. [Nicklaus's habit of imagining the task before he actually carried it out is a performance enhancement technique that is documented in psychological literature. Here is one such supportive study.]

Eugenio A. Peluso, *Skilled Motor Performance As a Function of Types of Mental Imagery.* Journal of Psychological Inquiry, Vol. 5, p. 11. Participants, 48 volunteers from introductory psychology classes, were assigned to either of two treatment groups or to a control group. Skilled motor performance was assessed by the number of errors and the speed with which participants performed pick-up jacks and mirror tracing tasks. Between trials, participants engaged in either relevant imagery (i.e., the tasks), irrelevant imagery (i.e., scenic environments), or no imagery. Following five imagery sessions, participants in the relevant imagery group committed significantly fewer errors than those in the other groups....These findings were consistent with a similar study using 40 novice table tennis players (Lejeune et al., 1994), which indicated that imagining oneself completing a sports skill in the absence of the actual movement increased the probability of improving one's performance.

50. Tiger putts to a picture
Woods, *Training a Tiger: A Father's Guide to Raising a Winner in Both Golf and Life.* p. 62-63.

51. We change our language
René van der Veer and Jaan Valsiner (Ed.), *Vygotsky Reader.* Blackwell 1994. Eidetic images [mental images so vivid and detailed that they seem to be visible] tend to disappear during the transition to thinking in concepts....the meanings of words became more general and abstract. [However, Vygotsky believes this ability is not lost forever.] Visual thinking does not completely disappear from the intellectual life of the adolescent along with the appearance of abstract thinking. It only moves to another place, goes off into the fantasy sphere, partly undergoes a change under the influence of abstract thinking and then, like any other function, rises to a higher level.

52. Finally, you can apply mood layers

Peluso, *Skilled Motor Performance as a Function of Types of Mental Imagery.* p. 11. Many athletes believe that mental imagery involves only one sense, vision, but this conclusion is incorrect. Along with the visual sense, mental imagery encompasses one's auditory, tactile, and kinesthetic senses, and these cues act in concert to influences [sic] one's emotional condition. First, people use their visual sense to follow a tennis ball or to identify a goal in hockey. Second, they use their tactile sense to familiarize themselves with the feel of the tennis racquet or the hockey stick. Third, they use their kinesthetic sense to keep their balance on the court or in the rink. Fourth, participants use their auditory sense to listen to the tennis ball hitting the strings or a hockey puck collide off the stick. These sounds may assist a players' [sic] timing in setting up the next shot in a tennis match or assist a save by the goalie in a hockey game. Finally, one's emotional state can facilitate mental imagery. By recreating prior experiences of anger, anxiety, frustration, or joy, athletes can control or regulate these emotions during competition (Weinberg, 1988).

53. Associating taste…richer shot

Win Wenger and Richard Poe, *The Einstein Factor: A Proven New Method for Increasing Your Intelligence.* Rocklin, CA, Prima Pub., 1996, p. 42-43, and Dominic O'Brien, *Learn to Remember.* San Francisco, Chronicle Books, 2000. [Synesthesia is a condition in which two or more senses are linked together. In the most common form, known as grapheme (letters and digits)/color synesthesia, letters or numbers are perceived in colors. Other examples of sense combinations are music and color, or sound and shapes. Although normally considered to be a trait possessed only by certain individuals, some psychologists think it may be a skill that can be developed. Wenger and Poe suggest as much when they say there is value in "fudging" descriptions as follows:] In general, *the more you describe something, the more of it you get.* ....This is why fudging or making up parts of your description is okay. The fudging is a legitimate imaginative process.... [As for what contributes to a person's better memory, eight-time World Memory Champion Dominic O'Brien demonstrates that associative techniques can help. Many of those associations are made with the assistance of the five senses. So, clearly, imagination, memory and the five senses are all related in a synesthetic relationship beneficial to anyone who wants to develop it through the practice of association.]

54. A gut-wrenching experience

Mihaly Csikszentmihalyi, *Flow: The Psychology of Optimal Experience.* New York, Harper & Row, 1990, p. 3. Contrary to what we usually believe, moments like these, the best moments in our lives, are not the passive, receptive, relaxing times – although such experiences can also be enjoyable, if we have worked hard to attain them. The best moments usually occur when a person's body or mind is stretched to its limits in a voluntary effort to accomplish something difficult and worthwhile....Such experiences are not necessarily pleasant at the time they occur. The swimmer's muscles might have ached during his most memorable race, his lungs might have felt like exploding, and he might have been dizzy with fatigue.

55. Characteristics of zone experience

Csikszentmihalyi, *Flow: The Psychology of Optimal Experience.* p. 49.

56. Firing at flags tucked into corners

Csikszentmihalyi, *Flow: The Psychology of Optimal Experience.* p. 97. [In the process of enjoying a zone experience, Kip raised the bar as he went along.] Even the simplest physical act becomes enjoyable when it is transformed so as to produce flow. The essential steps in this process are: (a) to set an overall goal, and as many sub-goals as are realistically feasible; (b) to find ways of measuring progress in terms of the goals chosen; (c) to keep concentrating on what one is doing, and to keep making finer and finer distinctions in the challenges involved in the activity; (d) to develop the skills necessary to interact with the opportunities available; and (e) to keep raising the stakes if the activity becomes too boring.

57. Giving up a few yards

Walter Mischel, Yuichi Shoda and Monica L. Rodriguez, *Delay of Gratification in Children.* Science, May 1989, Vol. 244, p. 933. To function effectively, individuals must voluntarily postpone immediate gratification and persist in goal-directed behavior for the sake of later outcomes....Studies in which 4-year-old children attempt this type of future-oriented self-control reveal that...individual differences in delay behavior significantly predict patterns of competence and coping assessed more than a decade later.... [In golf, trying to hit a drive as far as possible after a disappointment or frustration is a more immediate response than the delayed, self-disciplined approach of trying to place it in the correct position to set up the next shot. The latter can be seen as a way of delaying gratification – attaining a lower score – versus venting frustration or anger.]

58. Tiger focuses only on what he can control
Woods, *How I Play Golf.* p. 225-227.

59. Small details for Tiger
Woods, *How I Play Golf.* p. 225.

60. Finding fewer swing keys
Locke and Latham, *The Application of Goal Setting to Sports.* p. 212. Goals During Competition....The athlete should not be burdened by goal overload. People can only remember so much at once, and this capacity is reduced under conditions of stress. Thus, competitive goals should be limited to one or two important elements

61. It just doesn't get any better than this
Nicklaus, *My Story.* p. 368. [In the 1977 British Open at Turnberry, Jack Nicklaus and Tom Watson played what many people regard as the greatest head-to-head battle in golf of all time. They shot 65, 66 and 65, 65 respectively over the final two rounds. While there could only be one winner, it appears they both enjoyed how each pushed the other to a higher level. This is what Nicklaus had to say about the experience.] [I] increased my lead to two strokes with a good birdie at the twelfth hole. Tom then came right back at me again with a birdie at thirteen. On the fourteenth tee our glances happened to coincide for a moment and he said, "This is what it's all about, isn't it, Jack?" He couldn't have put it better, and I told him, "You're darn right."

62. Stimpmeter
[A stimpmeter is a metal track used to measure the speed of greens. A ball is released from a notch in one end of the track in response to that end being slowly raised by hand, while the other end rests on the ground. The distance the ball rolls onto the green from the track is measured. The average of two readings taken in opposite directions is the stimpmeter reading of the green on a particular day. Readings between 9.5 and 10.5 are common and reasonably fast. A reading of 11.5 is near the upper limit of playability.]

63. **Shooting 62**

USGA. [Last accessed December 15, 2006.] http://www.usga.org/> championships> U.S. Amateur> Archives> 2006. [A score of 62 is quite realistic in today's world of golf. Consider these career-low competitive scores of quarterfinalists in the 2006 U.S. Amateur, as well as one of the scores in medal qualifying play.]

- 61, by Trip Kuehne, Dallas, Texas

- 62, on four occasions by Rickie Fowler, Murrieta, California

- 62, at Murcur Golf Club, by Richard Ramsay, Aberdeen, Scotland

- 63, at Indian Canyon, by Alex Prugh, Spokane, Washington

- 63, at the Dogwood Amateur, by Webb Simpson, Raleigh, North Carolina

- 63, at the MAC championship, by Ryan Yip, Calgary, Alberta

- 60, in the first round of medal play at the 2006 U.S. Amateur, by Billy Horschel, 19, Grant, Florida

BIBLIOGRAPHY

If printed here, the bibliography for this book would stretch to 10 pages, or a full five percent of the length of the book. Interestingly, today's cyber world offers an opportunity for its presentation that has not always been available to readers and authors. Not only can all of the sources be listed without concern for space, but also an electronic version allows readers to link to many of them with the click of a mouse. Therefore, the bibliography of this book can be found at http://www.howgreatgolfersthink.com/. I'm sure that this format will be the preferred option for those who wish to delve further into my research about how great golfers, and other great people, think.

Bob Skura

Notes

Notes

Notes

Notes

Notes

ABOUT THE AUTHOR

After graduating from the University of Waterloo, Bob Skura taught and played professional golf for five years. Later he developed a career in sales, becoming the proprietor of his own successful company. Bob's athletic and professional experience have taught him that, with the correct approach, our potential to improve all areas of our lives is almost unlimited. In this book, he demonstrates how great achievers use sound psychological principles as a template for their successes, and how anyone can emulate them.

In addition to playing competitive golf, Bob enjoys riding his unicycle and juggling, two skills he developed after the age of 50. He brings this same lighthearted, no-boundaries approach to *How Great Golfers Think*. Bob lives in Kitchener, Ontario, with his wife, Sharon, and can be reached at:

doc@howgreatgolfersthink.com
www.howgreatgolfersthink.com